Dear Colin,

from

Also by Peter Shergold

The War in Northern Oman (Hellion & Co)

Home Front – A History of Britain at War and 6th (Sutton) Battalion
Warwickshire Home Guard (Boldmere Press)

Carry On Sergeant Major

The story of
Company Sergeant Major
Thomas Charles Craddock MM
7th Battalion South Staffordshire Regiment

Boldmere Press
Birmingham
Text Copyright © 2023

The right of Peter Shergold to be identified as the Author of the work has been asserted by him in accordance with the Copyright, Designs and Patents Act 1988.

Published by Boldmere Press Limited

Apart from any use permitted under UK copyright law, this publication may only be reproduced, stored or transmitted, in any form, or by any means, with prior permission in writing of the publishers or, in the case of reprographic production, in accordance with the terms of licences issued by the Copyright Licencing Agency.

All picture credits © Boldmere Press Limited

Every effort has been made to fulfil requirements with regard to reproducing copyright material. The author and publisher will be glad to rectify any omissions at the earliest opportunity.

Printed and bound in Great Britain by Amazon

ISBN 979 8 8628 7519 5

BOLDMERE PRESS LIMITED
Boldmere
Royal Sutton Coldfield
B73 6NP

Contents

Introduction

Glossary

Chapter 1 – Walsall

Chapter 2 – Home Service

Chapter 3 – Gallipoli

Chapter 4 – Home Front

Chapter 5 – France 1916

Chapter 6 – 1917

Chapter 7 – Passchendaele

Chapter 8 – Trench Raid

Chapter 9 – 1918

Chapter 10 – Epilogue

Annex A – Battalion Locations

Annex B – Formation Commanders

Annex C – Known Officers of The Battalion - Appointments

Annex D – Known Warrant Officers of The Battalion - Appointments

Annex E – Known Officers of The Battalion - All Officers

Annex F – Casualties of the 7th Battalion

Annex G – Lt Col W H Carter

Annex H – Bibliography

Introduction

During the First World War over six million men served with the British Army. It grew from a professional force over around 250,000 men to millions flocking to the colours to serve King and Empire. Of those who served, around a million were killed. The war's impact upon British society is shown through the memorials in almost every town and village across the country. It is a visible legacy that has carved itself upon the sole of a nation. To this day each November the nation remembers the silencing of the guns.

The men who fought in this war came from many backgrounds, and like any army, represented the society they lived in. The war took place at the height of the British Empire, with a polarised class system which is reflected in much of the literature of the period. In many ways, although the army did contain many from the upper echelons of society, or the Victorian middle class, the mass of the army were those from working backgrounds and from the industrial urban areas, where the majority of the population now lived.

It was the Regimental system in which these soldiers, who would join for front line service would be a part of; a system of recruitment locally which has existed in some form since the 16th Century. The association with counties came later, when in 1871 this was seen as a good method of increasing recruitment and aligning to depots. The structure of the British Army also changed over time, but local militia, later territorial forces were always a feature, to allow for the defence of the United Kingdom whilst the regular forces were deployed overseas.

At the turn of the 20th Century, Walsall was in an era of economic boom, with its huge leather trade and heavy industry, as part of the wider Black Country, bringing impressive wealth to the city. Over the previous century, large numbers of people had moved into the town from the surrounding countryside. In a time of low paid work, with long hours and difficult conditions, the populations used territorial service as an additional income, as much if not more, than any nationalistic affiliation of serving their country.

Walsall at this time was in the county of Staffordshire, and despite being at the far southern edge of the county and having much more in common with its large neighbour Birmingham, it was proud of its preindustrial county roots. When soldiers reported to duty, it was to the South Staffordshire Regiment they would flock. The territorial battalions and companies were spread across the urban areas, recruiting from these industrial towns, under the guise of national defence. In reality, they served a different purpose, overseas, when the war came.

The records of the period are not complete, with many being destroyed during bombing in the Second World War. The Regimental War Diary of the 7th Battalion South Staffordshire Regiment is at the bottom of the Mediterranean Sea, sunk on its way to Egypt after the battalion left the peninsular. The niece of Thomas Craddock learned his story as a young girl and told her family about it, so some of the stories are told from family legend. Through these incomplete records a story emerges of a man who not only served his time, but excelled, becoming the senior soldier, the Sergeant Major.

I would like to thank my family for letting me dig into our past to learn about this story and where part of our family came from. I would also like to thank particularly my mom and dad who kept records of the time, including some recordings of interviews with my great grandmother, and postcards from the war. And as always, I would like to thank my wife, Laura for being there for me and letting me write away in the evenings. I would also like to that Isabelle for checking my work with her usual diligence.

This book is about one soldier who served during the First World War in this South Staffordshire Regiment. It is a journey through the military systems of the day, and the societal changes which occurred through this period. I hope it brings to life one story, in a period of history which should never be forgotten.

PJD Shergold
October 2023

x

Glossary and Abbreviations

General Commanding. A commanding officer of a British Formation, a Division, Corps or Army. Rank of Major General or above.

Brigade Commander. The commander of a Brigade, a group of battalions and a tactical fighting formation.

Commanding Officer. The person in charge of a British Battalion, also called a Regiment.

Officer. A person who holds the King's commission and has a commissioned rank. Usually in charge of soldiers but can also be in an administrative or staff role.

Warrant Officer. The holder of a Kings Warrant, and the senior rank that a soldier can gain without commission.

Senior NCO. A senior non-commissioned officer, either a Sergeant or a Colour Sergeant.

Junior NCO. A Junior non-commissioned officer, either a Corporal or Lance Corporal. In 1914 and 1915 the rank of Corporal was called Lance Sergeant or Lance Serjeant.

Platoon. The smallest unit commanded by an officer, normally of lieutenant, and containing up to fifty men. Can be broken into sections.

Company. The smallest independent subunit of the British Army, containing around 200 men, and commanded by a Captain.

Battalion. An independent unit with all its support elements within it, making it able to operate across the conflict. Containing four rifle companies, and a headquarters company. Made up of around a thousand men and commanded by a Lieutenant Colonel.

Brigade. A group of four battalions (three from 1917), commanded by a Brigadier General.

Division. A group of three to six Brigades structured for combat and commanded by a Major General.

Corps. A group of Divisions commanded by a Lieutenant General.

Army. The largest tactical formation, structured into a series of Corps.

Sap. A trench dug out of the side of another trench, to extend its length, or to allow movement closer to the enemy.

Trench. A ditch dug to protect men from enemy fire.

Dug Out. A whole in the ground dug to conduct administration in. These can vary from the size of two men cut into the side of a trench, to a large bunker dug under the ground for many hundreds of people.

Lewis Gun. An early machine gun.

P Bomb. A phosphorous hand threw bomb.

Gas Shell. A poison gas shell, of various types.

Mobile charges. A large explosive charge, used to destroy trenches, bunkers and dug outs, which could be carried.

Looting parties. Groups of men tasked to capture enemy equipment on a raid.

Stretcher bearers. Men tasked to carry the wounded.

Runners. Men tasked to run between commanders and pass messages.

H-Hour. The start time of an operation.

D-Day. The start day of an operation.

Chapter 1
Walsall

Mary Ann Brown was born in the village of Rothley in Leicestershire. Like many in Victorian Britain, she moved to an urban area because of work and her family chose Walsall, which at the time has an insatiable demand for workers in its leather industry. Mary moved as a young girl to Butts Road, which was just outside of Walsall town centre in the old mining village of Rushall, with her family. Rushall was no longer a village, but part of a wider conurbation joining all of the local areas into one urban mass (in 1980 this area would formally become part of Walsall). Long terrace houses had been constructed for workers, and it was in one of these small terraces which the family would live. In 1855 Hatherton Place was described as a pleasant little street with particularly beautiful houses, while the Littleton Street area was one 'where streets and habitations are daily springing up on every side'. In the centre of Walsall, Hatherton, Teddesley, and Upper Forster Streets run into the area known as the Butts, which was added to Walsall from Rushall in 1876 but had been part of the Walsall improvement commissioners' district from 1848. Lord Hatherton granted leases in the area from 1840, and a working-class district grew up. A school was opened in 1868 and a mission chapel in 1871.

Mary was the second oldest child in her family, after her brother Charles. She was lucky to not be working and to have some time in school, because Charles, even at age seven, was working as a window boy. At the age of 15 in 1861, Mary did start work, becoming a live-in servant for the Thacker family, who lived at 33 Field Gate, New Street, on Walsall Foreign. William Thacker & Sons were manufactures of equestrian equipment, leather goods for horses. Leather work was a huge industry in Walsall, and even provided goods to the

Royal Family. The work would have been hard, with long hours, and with such a large family in the house, quite a difficult life for such a young girl.

Life changed in her mid-twenties for Mary when she met and then married James Cradock in 1867. James was a tanner working in the same industry as the Thacker family. They moved into a small house at 40 Butts Road. This was just over the road from Mary's mother and would have been a nice place to live so close to other family. Within two years, the couple had two children, Emma and Sarah Ann. They also brought in a lodger, Charlotte Crutchley, who was a 53-year-old laundry worker, who helped with the housework, and brough in a little income for the family.

Over the nineteenth century, the population of Walsall had grown almost tenfold, with hundreds of people moving to the town, with its rapidly expanding industry. Walsall had grown in 60 years from a village of 5,000 people to an industrial town of 86,000 people. Improved to the quality of life of the population continued as the town became wealthier. The 'Walsall Improvement and Market Act' was passed in 1848 and amended in 1850. The act provided facilities for the poor, improving and extending the sewerage system and giving the commissioners the powers to construct a new gas works.

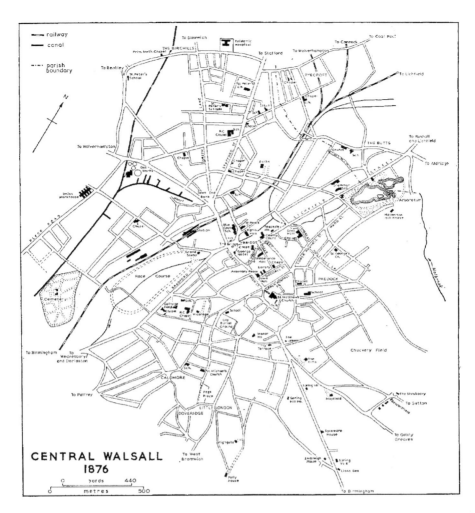

Image 1: Map of Central Walsall 1876 (Walsall Archive)

The area to the north of the arboretum was partly in Rushall until 1876. Limestone was being quarried there by the late 18th century but operations had ceased by the earlier 1840s, leaving two flooded pits, the larger of which was known as Hatherton Lake. In 1858 it was suggested that a public park should be made in the area and from 1868 Lord Hatherton's agent was supporting the idea as a means of improving the locality and encouraging development. The Walsall Arboretum and Lake Company was formed in

1870, and in 1873 it took a lease from Lord Hatherton and Sir George Mellish of the two lakes the land was to be laid out as 'an arboretum or pleasure grounds and gardens'. The park was opened in 1874, giving a space for the public to relax and play and escape from the dirt and hustle of the town. Butts Road was just off the northern edge of the arboretum, so the family were able to take a walk across the park, after their Sunday service at the church. The Hatherton Arms was the local pub also, which James popped into after a hard day at the leather factory, when he had the money.

By 1881 the family, still living at 40 Butts Street, had expanded further with Emma now 12, there was also Sarah age 10, Eliza age 8, Joseph age 5, James Ezra age 3 and baby Ellen. There was also a niece called Sarah, aged 10, who lived with the family. All of the children went to school at this time, a thing which would never have been heard of in their mother's day. Thomas Charles Craddock was born on the 22nd December 1884 at the family home at Number 40 Butts Street, Rushall. He was the sixth child born to Mary and James.

Ten years later, the family had moved again to number 5 Butts Lane and had grown further, with four more children, Louise, Thomas, Mary and Frank-William, there was also a granddaughter, Lilly. Eliza was now a machinist at the leather factory, and Joseph was a saddler. The younger children were at school, although Thomas aged seven was not. James and Mary now had ten children and one grandchild, a huge number of mouths to feed, but a normal size family for the day. By 1897 the Victorian arcade had been contructed in Walsall, giving the town centre a grand appearance. Such improvements and beautification of the town were the pinnacle of Victorian development. The central library was opened in 1906 and public baths had been opened behind the library site in 1896.

At the turn of the century, one more boy was born, Robert. Six children and one grandchild lived in the small house on lower Whitehouse Street with James, but the marriage of James and Mary was not what it used to be, and Mary had found her own way by becoming a nurse to an eighty-year-old lady, Maria Thomlinson, in a large house of Mr Frederick Ravenhill, who lived at 14 High Road, next to the Dragon Hotel on 'The Bridge' in the centre of town. James lived with three sons and a daughter. The sons all worked with him in the leather factory and the daughter Mary now 23 looked after the home. Mary lived at 64 Mill Lane with her son Thomas who was now 16 and an apprentice leather worker.

Thomas lived with his mother for the subsequent years and tried to earn money to support her in her newfound independence. In 1908 a new opportunity for income appeared in the form of the new Territorial Force. The promise of regular additional payment and a bounty was very attractive.

The new Territorial Force was created for the British Army to provide the defence of the British Isles if the regular army were deployed abroad. The Force was deigned to reinforce the army overseas in case of expeditionary operations, but the volunteers could not be compelled to serve overseas, and therefore they were mainly a home defence organisation, and were liable for service anywhere in the United Kingdom. The Territorial force consisted of 204 infantry battalions, divided into 14 territorial divisions each of three brigades. There were commanded through the War Office but administrated by the local County Territorial Associations.

Thomas signed up to serve in this new force, he signed up for the 5th Battalion of the Royal Warwickshire Regiment, based out of the drill hall in Thorpe Street Birmingham (next to the Hippodrome). It is not known why Thomas decided to join the 5th Warwickshire Regiment, rather than the Staffordshire Battalion based in Walsall, but the motivations could have been friendships, work, or even as simple as this battalion was recruiting at the time. Whatever the reasons, at the age of 24, he volunteered for a four-year term of service in the territorials under the Military Service Act. At the end of this period, Thomas 'time expired' and this was reflected on this service record. As a territorial solider, he was entitled to pay at army rates, and therefore this provided Thomas with additional income in his spare time.

Prior to the formation of the Territorial Force, the 5th Battalion, Royal Warwickshire Regiment had a long history as the 1st Battalion of the Birmingham Rifles. Originally formed in 1859 as part of the Rifle Volunteer Corps, the battalion had at its peak 12 companies across the city of Birmingham, and two deployed during the Boar War. Later the Battalion became the 1st Volunteer Battalion of the regiment on 1 January 1883 of the Royal Warwickshire Regiment giving it a county affiliation. The Territorial Yearbook for 1909 records that the 5th Battalion strength comprised 24 officers and 808 men.

Recruits were required to attend a minimum of 40 drill periods in their first year and 20 per year thereafter. All members were required to attend between 8 and 15 days of annual camp. Drill nights consisted of marching and rifle drill, which included all the elements of cleaning, assembly and working their weapon systems. This week in, week out training was designed to give them knowledge and proficiency in their roles. The annual tented camp then allowed all of the local units to join together and allow more large-scale tactical training.

In 1911, Thomas was now 26 and a caster, working for T L Hale in Hatherton Road. T. L Hale was headquartered at Dudley Port in Tipton and were makers of malleable iron and steel alloy castings. They provided a large contract to J Reeves and Sons, which were a large art and design firm. This job for Thomas was a semi-skilled labourer role, which allowed him to support his mother in their small house. Next door at 66 lived Thomas's sister Ellen who was now married to Albert and had her own family. The whole Craddock family lived in this small area, with the Hatherton Arms at its centre. It was a tight knit community despite the huge population expansion in the area. Thomas was on the path to starting a career, and maybe even a family, but dark clouds lay ahead in the near future.

8

Chapter 2

Home Service

The First World War broke out on 4th August 1914, with Great Britain declaring war on Germany after its invasion of neutral Belgium. The British armed forces mobilised for war, with the regular army moving to France, formed as the British Expeditionary Force. The mobilisation of the army was a considerable undertaking, with Regular Reserve troops, those who had completed their term in the military, recalled to service with the Colours and joining to bring regular battalions up to full strength. In addition, the Territorial Force was mobilised, however those territorial soldiers were not compelled to serve overseas, so the territorial battalions were divided into two units, with the first unit preparing to deploy overseas, and the second unit mobilised for home defence. Such was the case with Thomas's old battalion the 5th Battalion Royal Warwickshire Regiment, which formed the 1/5th Battalion Royal Warwickshire Regiment for overseas service and 2/5th for home defence.

Thomas in 1914 was still employed as a caster by Messrs T. L. Hale, in Hatherton Street, Walsall. His father James was living at 25 Wallhouse Street and his mother Mary at 67 Mill Lane at this time, with Thomas. He was single and as he was working in an important industry, a key worker, he would have felt little pressure to have signed up to the military. However, Thomas was nationalistic in his outlook, and based on his prior military service in the Territorial Force, he decided to sign up, along with tens of thousands of others at this time of national mobilisation. Thomas enlisted in the army on 11th August 1914 in Walsall. After a medical which described him as 5 foot 5 ¼ inches tall, with good vision and a chest of 37 inches, he was made Private 8711 in the 5th (Territorial) Battalion South Staffordshire Regiment.

Unlike his prior Territorial Service in Birmingham with the 5th Battalion, the Warwickshire Regiment, Thomas decided to sign up locally to the Whittimere Street drill hall. In 1866, Whittimere Street drill hall in Walsall was constructed. The building was designed as the headquarters of the 3rd Staffordshire Rifle Volunteer Corps. This unit evolved to become the 2nd Volunteer Battalion, the South Staffordshire Regiment in 1885 and the 5th Battalion, the South Staffordshire Regiment in 1908. The militia unit was formed on the back of invasion scares in mid Victorian Britain, but would form the basis of future developments which would eventually lead to the formation of the Territorial Force in the early 20th Century. Many workers in the town volunteered for the militia, as a source of extra income.

The 5th (Territorial) Battalion South Staffordshire Regiment mobilised in Walsall with many soldiers parading in the town centre to watch the troops form up in their full equipment. In the photo of the battalion on parade taken in the town centre, a small girl can be seen in a white dress on the shoulders of her father. Elizabeth May Evans, was the daughter of Thomas' sister Ellan and her husband Albert, and she remembered that day sitting on the fathers shoulders cheering her uncle as he went to war. With a magnifying glass you can see her there in her dress watching the men on parade.

Image 2: 5th South Staffordshire Regiment 11th August 1914, Walsall town centre being addressed by the Mayor (Authors Collection)

The battalion moved to be encamped in the Luton Area, to form part of the Staffordshire Brigade of the North Midland Division. There was a huge formation of Territorial Forces from across the Midlands, with thousands of men ready and equipped to go to war. The soldiers stayed in their tented camp and conducted daily drills and fitness to get them ready for war. After two weeks in the camp, the war office announced a policy on the future of the Territorial Force. They were asked if they wished to serve overseas or not, and this led to the formation of the 1/5th for overseas service, which Thomas joined. Those who did not volunteer joined the 2/5th which became part of the 2nd Staffordshire Brigade, 2nd Midland Division. This 2/5th would move to Luton also by January 1915, then St Albans, before being posted to Ireland for the disturbances of 1916. In 1917 this unit would be compelled to serve overseas, but this would be after three years of war.

At first, the war in France went badly for the British, with large scale battles across Belgium and a retreat towards Mons. Between September and December, there was a solidification of the defensive lines and the start of what would be known as trench warfare. With the huge losses in manpower, it was decided that the volunteer Territorial Force would be deployed to France to reinforce the British Expeditionary Force. In November 1914, the 1/5th (Territorial) Battalion South Staffordshire Regiment moved to Bishops Stortford to prepare for deployment to France. The training was intense, but it was not to be in the first wave of deployments, landing on 3rd March 1915.

However, for Thomas the war took a different path and on 5th December 1914 at Safron Waldon, Thomas was discharged as medically unfit from the army after 116 days on home service. This discharge was under paragraph 156(11) of Territorial regulations in that he was medically unfit for service. The reasons for this unfitness are not recorded, however this was confirmed on 15th April 1915 at Lichfield, the Regimental Depot where Thomas had been sent back to in order to demobilise. At the age of thirty, Thomas was not the youngest of soldiers, and after a hard life working as a castor and in the poorer area of Walsall, he was not in the best of health. Authority has been given for battalions to discharge men who went sick for more than two days, without any further course. This focus on quality soldiers, showed how well off the army was at this point for soldiers in terms of sheer numbers.

Thomas returned to work as a castor and lived again with his family who were hugely pleased to see him safe, especially his little niece Elizabeth. But the life of a worker in Britain at the time was not easy, with long hard six-day war weeks, and an expectation to support the home front. There were also now shortages of food and items in shops as the German *unterseeboots* started to impact in their blockade of Britain, times were getting very difficult.

The war also changed forever in January 1915, when on the night of the 19th two Zeppelins appeared over Norfolk and bombed a number of coastal towns, killing four people and injuring sixteen. The war had reached the home front, and a new threat which affected people's families was now a reality. On the back of these threats, many Volunteer Training Corps were formed, with people determined to do their bit for the home front and defend their homes from the perceived invasion threat.

All these difficulties, and a growth in nationalism, led to the rise of the White Feather movement. The Order of the White Feather was founded as a propaganda campaign to shame men into signing up to join the fight, thus associating the white feather with cowardice and dereliction of duty. With the White Feather movement gaining greater traction, any young Englishman that the women would deem an eligible proposition for the army, could be handed the white feather, with the aim of humiliating and defaming the individuals, compelling them to enlist. Often, many of the women also misjudged their targets, with many men who were on leave from service being handed a white feather.

Such pressures were very difficult for a man not in the forces. In addition, as the war continued into 1915 and became a stalemate, the drive for additional soldiers to form infantry for the Western Front led to a huge recruitment campaign. The famous Kitchener campaign to form new armies has recruited over half a million men in the first few months of the war, but the scale of the conflict led to a huge expansion of the British Army and therefore a need to get more and more volunteers signed up.

With the need, came a lowering of standards and often doctors were urged to be less meticulous when recruiting and not ask too many questions. When Thomas tried to sign up again in January 1915, he was successful, joining under a new army number as Private 17778 Thomas Charles Craddock. Thomas again decided to join his local regiment, but this time the 7th (Service) Battalion South Staffordshire Regiment, part of the first Kitchener Army (K1). The battalion was full of volunteers who were new to the army and not tied down by the Territorial Force restrictions on home service.

At the outbreak of war the decision was made to form 'Service Battalions' made up of volunteers who would sign up for war time service. On 15th August 1914, 2000 men stood on the square at the depot of the South Staffordshire Regiment in Whittington and were divided into two battalions, many of these soldiers were from the local mining villages, and were in good physical shape. Officers from the Territorial Force and Regular Army were allocated to the battalion, and three regular Sergeants were sent to assist in training. Sergeants Armstrong, Jardine and Tresise joined the battalion fro the 1st Battalion The South Staffordshire Regiment, in addition a number of retired Senior Non Commissioned Officers had rejoined, these included Colour Sergeants Munn and Hill as well as Sergeants Hill, Jones, Barnbrook, Barnes, Balance and Barratt. This helped to bring order to the battalion and allow initial training to start.

Initially for training the battalion, many different public buildings such as schools and churches were used in response to the need for more adequate training spaces. Eventually purpose-built training camps were developed, and original barracks expanded. From September 1914 Belton Park, Grantham in Lincolnshire had been set aside for the training of Kitchener's new army. The Earl Brownlow placed the whole of his family estate available for the army as a camping and training ground for the duration of the war. It was here than a full training programme started for the new recruits and Thomas, as an experienced Territorial Force soldier was quickly spotted as a leader of men and given a role of mentoring the newer soldiers in his company.

From the 28th August 1914, the 7th (Service) Battalion South Staffordshire Regiment were training at Belton Park as part of the 33rd Brigade, 11th Northern Division. Thousands of soldiers from the new army were living in the tented encampment. Time was spent over the winter doing sports, light training and route marches. The longest march the battalion did was a 52 mile round trip in one day, with only two men falling out. The weather was bad, and the descriptions of the camp were of a sea of mud, with little social activity other than that provided by the YMCA hut.

The battalion was commanded initially by Major Daukes, who would soon be promoted to Lieutenant Colonel, a reservist who had been appointed to the role. The second in command was Major Pipe-Wolferstan, but this officer was quickly promoted and Major Yool took over the appointment. The Adjutant was initially Captain Richie, but again rapid promotion led to Captain Morris to take over this role. Sergeant Major Cawap was the first Regimental Sergeant Major, but was soon taken over by Sergeant Major Mee. The command team by Christmas was more stable, with most roles in the battalion filled with experience commanders, many with experience in the regular army.

Image 3: Visit of The King at Frensham Camp (Authors Collection)

In April 1915, the battalion moved to Frensham in Surrey for their final pre-embarkation training. The small village had a population of only 3,000 people prior to the war, but had ballooned as the holding camp had been placed here, near to the main train line at Farnham. While at the training camps, the soldiers were put through their paces with physical fitness training, as well as marching and drills. At this final camp, the battalion were taught 'modern warfare' techniques, including the use of hand grenades and the placing of barbed wire. In April a trench system was dug by the Brigade and throughout May and June inter-divisional fighting took place over this.

After three months of training in Frensham, the battalion was visited by the King and Queen on their tour of the camp. On the 29th June the battalion were informed that they would be posted to Gallipoli. On the day of departure, Captain Morris the Adjutant fell from his horse and would deploy to war with his arm in a sling. The battalion then moved by train across England to the port of Liverpool, where they embarked on a troop ship MHT Empress of Britain to Alexandria with three destroyer escorts. The soldiers enjoyed the salt baths on the ship, and the experience of cool beer from a refrigerator. The ship stopped at Malta to coal on route, and the soldiers were impressed by the sign of the Dreadnought HMS Lion. At Alexandria the soldiers stayed on board in port for three days, which was very disappointing. However, on the third day the soldiers were allowed on shore for a training route march. The convoy left for Mudros in Greece where they left the battalion echelon. On 20th July 1915, the battalion moved in on the Italian Coaster Abushai to 'V' Beach at Cape Helles.

18

Chapter 3
Gallipoli

The attempt by the allied forces to attack the soft underbelly of Europe, started in February 1916 with an assault by the combined naval forces of France, Britain and Russia to seize the Ottoman Straits. The strategy was to cause the Ottoman capital Constantinople to be cut off from Asia and to be able to be bombarded the city by sea. With the Ottoman Empire being knocked out of the war, the Suez would be secure, and supplies could be transported to Russia via the Black Sea. However, despite such bold intentions, the attempts by allied naval forces the straight was defeated, with the loss of a number of ships.

Because of this failure, an amphibious landing on the Gallipoli peninsula was planned for April 1915. The initial assaults made limited progress, and static trench warfare follow in the most difficult dry mountainous conditions. The 7th Battalion South Staffordshire Regiment landed in the rear of the army on the small Italian Coaster Abushai with 33rd Infantry Brigade. The remainder of the 11th Infantry Division landed at Mudros awaiting orders. On route into the beach area the boat was slightly shelled, and a small ship containing flairs was hit, lighting up the whole scene.

The battalion unloaded and moved up to the reserve park where they had five hours sleep. They then moved up to the reserve trenches on 24th July, taking over from the 9th Sherwood Foresters on the slopes of Achi Baba. This takeover was a brutal induction to trench warfare, the trench terraces had been built up from dead soldier from both sides. The Naval Division based in the trenches were riddled with disease and fatigue. On the move forward to the horseshoe where they were to be based, the first officer was killed, 2nd

Lieutenant Somerton, the battalion Scout Officer, was killed by a sniper. Captain Hume was hit in the spine by a ricochet and died on his way back to England. During this short period in reserve, the battalion lost two officers and two soldiers, with nine soldiers wounded.

On 28th July the battalion was relieved and orders were received to re-embark on the 1st August and prepare for a landing at Suvla Bay. After four months of fighting in Gallipoli, a second assault was planned to take place on Suvla Bay, and it was planned that the 7th Battalion South Staffordshire Regiment would form part of the assault. The battalion sailed on the SS Osmaneih to the Island of Imbros and prepared for the assault.

The 11th Division, commanded by Major General Sir Edward Fanshawe, consisted of the 32nd and 33rd Infantry Brigades. The 33rd Brigade contained four infantry battalions, the 6th Battalion Lincolnshire Regiment, the 6th Battalion Border Regiment, 9th Battalion Sherwood Foresters and the 7th Battalion South Staffordshire Regiment. In addition, the Brigade contained the 33rd Machine Gun Company in support. All of these units were 'Service Battalions' of Kitchener's New Army, unproven in battle. Thomas Craddock was now in A Company of the 7th Battalion South Staffordshire Regiment, part of the follow-on assault units which were to come ashore at 'B Beach' just south of Nibrunesi Point, at 10am on 7th August 1916.

It was planned that the 7th Battalion South Staffordshire Regiment would come ashore to a beachhead which had been secured in the night, and conduct a forward passage of lines, securing the high ground inland. A, B and D Companies landed on two lighters towed by destroyers under the command of Major Yool, and in conjunction with three companies of the 9th Sherwood Foresters. The landing for the 11th Division in pitch darkness had become chaotic, with many units getting lost and missing their objectives. Ottoman snipers targeted the British as they landed, causing further chaos in the inexperienced British ranks. Although the first objective 'Hill 10' had been taken, this was due to the Ottomans withdrawing rather than any feet of arms.

However, the landing of the 7th Battalion had been uneventful, with only a few Turks firing and running away after, although Lieutenant Thomson was wounded. They moved inland and dug in on a line from 'Salt lake' to the sea. The next morning, a number of patrols were sent forward, with two men being killed, but the main actions were with other units of the division. The battalion was mainly focused on digging trenches and defensive positions. A, B and D Companies were in the front line, C Company in reserve. There was a huge amount of dysentery across the battalion due to eating fruit and vegetables whilst in Imbros. Orders were then received for an attack on the morning of 9th August.

The battalion woke at 3am on the 9th and moved to its assembly area by 4am, just northwest of chocolate hill. Whilst moving forward Captain Cowap was wounded in the head. The battalion objective was Anafarta village, 1500 yards to the front, which was to be assaulted by 6th Border Regiment on the left, 7th South Staffordshire Regiment in the centre and 6th Lincoln Regiment on the right. At 5am the advance started, but quickly was held back by heavy fire and counterattacks. There was overlapping of the lead units of the 7th South Staffords and the 6th Lincolns, with Major Yool moving forward to try and untangle them. However at 6am as the battalion reached Hill 70 they came under a huge weight of Ottoman artillery fire, with the shrapnel inflicting many casualties. Within minutes every officer in A, B and D Company were killed or wounded. Major Yool continued forward with a bullet in his arm but was then shot in the leg. The soldiers were caught in the open, and by 10am the scrub bushes caught alight wounding many on the ground further with horrid burns.

The battalion suffered considerably, losing the commanding officer Lieutenant Colonel Archibald Daukes and many soldiers. On the day, 44 men were reported killed and 206 men wounded, which was later revised to 119 men killed, including five Captains and six Lieutenants, with many more wounded. Such losses were devastating to the battalion's ability to function with both the Commanding Officer, and the Adjutant killed, as well as many company officers. Captain Ransford took over command from the 10th to 13th August. The battalion held the line and quickly they were forced to dig trenches. Such digging was extremely difficult with the Ottomans firing from above, and the hard rock surfaces.

The battalion finally went firm in entrenched positions located on the southern edge of the Suvla sector, between the 'W' Hills in the south, and to the north Scimitar Hill, with its curved summit. Major E C P Bridges took command. These hills were to have been objectives on the first day of the assault, but now two weeks later the British had failed to reach them and planned an attack with both the 11th Division and the 10th (Irish) Division on 21st August. The 11th Division, led by the 7th South Staffordshire Regiment targeted the W Hills, but the assault failed due to the huge weight of artillery fire and machine guns from strong points. Forming up at 3.30pm, the Royal Navy bombarded Turkish positions, but heavy shell fire returned and within a short period of time all the officers of the battalion were wounded except for 2nd Lieutenant Miller and 2nd Lieutenant Hanner who had only joined the battalion two hours before the attack. The attack was the last attempt by the British to advance, and the front continued into stale mate for the next four months. 36 soldiers in the battalion were killed during the attempted assault, including Regimental

Sergeant Major Francis Henry Mee. 300 men were wounded. Up to the 28th August 2nd Lieutenant Miller and 2nd Lieutenant Hanner did their best to maintain the morale of the men, but they were exhausted, and 2nd Lieutenant Miller was shot in the leg again.

On the 24th, the battalion pulled back to the reserve trenches and was temporarily merged with the 9th Sherwood Foresters under Capt F S Duck 6 Lincoln Regt. Although it moved to the front line on the 28th, no further active operations were taken, and on 14th September, the battalion moved into reserve and reformed under the command of Major DT Seckham of 4th Battalion South Staffordshire Regiment. The fighting had been devastating to the battalion, with the loss of all the command elements, both in terms of Officers and Warrant Officers. The losses of soldiers were so heavy, that any cohesion of training in England prior to departure was lost, as well as much of the unit identity. From the 20th September, Lieutenant Colonel Seckham formed the battalion into two companies, A and B. The morale of the men was very poor, with their appearance being terrible, and weapons not cleaned. The quartermaster, despite suffering heavily from sickness, worked hard with Company Quartermasters Evans and Worker to maintain the spirit of the men with food and supplies. On the 26th September a new draft of soldiers arrived, including Company Sergeant Major Tosdevine of D Company, with the battalion now forming four companies again.

The battalion was completely reorganised, with draft of offers and men brought in in large numbers, however over the next four months, the constant trench warfare claimed a further 28 soldiers were killed in the battalion and 10 wounded. The summer conditions were very difficult for the soldiers, with high temperatures and little sanitation. Even getting basic supplies forward was difficult. Stores were in such short supply that men were restricted to three rounds of ammunition per day. On 10th October a draft of 150 men arrived, followed by 164 more men a few weeks later. Although the numbers were increasing, there were many non-battle casualties occurring, including men suffering from jaundice. The Adjutant and the Medical Officer suffered from this debilitating disease. In November, the weather turned to torrential rainfall, with trenches filling up to four feet deep.

On the night of 26th November, heavy rain broke down the parapet of A Company's trenches. The water carried everything in its path, destroying positions and exposing the men of Thomas' company to the enemy. On the 28th rain turned to snow and frost, with over 220 men in the British Army at Sulva drowning or freezing to death. The Turks suffered also, with men and horses washed over into the 7th Battalion's trenches. Water became difficult with the camel tanks that held it frozen up. 130 men of the battalion were sent away sick between the 26th and 30th November.

The battalion fought for four months before being evacuated as part of the general evacuation of the peninsular and failure of the campaign. On the 15th December the Brigade Commander, Brigadier General Hodson was wounded by a sniper, dying of his wounds. The new Brigade Commander was Brigadier General J Hill, who temporarily took over command for the evacuation from his permanent role in 24th Infantry Brigade. 400 men and 12 officers were evacuated on 18th December, and the remainder of the 20th. B Company held to the last and were last to leave of the entire Brigade. The last position, known as the 'post of honour' was held by Captain Grice, 2nd Lieutenants Charlton and Muscat for being the longest serving of the battalion. As the final party moved off, they were treated to a dramatic moment, with the Turks sending 6 shells towards the beach. Sulva was the final position to be evacuated, with the 7th Battalion South Staffordshire Regiment one of the last units to leave. With the poor weather, and close terrain, there was an expectation that there would be high casualties, around 20,000, but in the end only three were wounded. The battalion managed to retire with minimal loss. The final two soldiers to die on the campaign succumbed to their wounds after the evacuation. Corporal Charles Adams from Walsall, and Lance Corporal Alfred Clark were both buried at sea. At 03:30am the battalion sailed from the peninsular on the captured German ship Derfflinger.

The battalion had suffered considerably in the campaign, throughout the difficult fighting against the Turks 213 were killed and many more wounded. The British Army had almost 250,000 casualties during the campaign. 13 officers were killed, including the commanding officer, and adjutant. Sixteen senior NCOs were killed including the regimental sergeant major, and one company sergeant major. Forty-two Junior NCOs were killed and 142 privates. On top of these losses, many more were wounded, leading to a battalion which was a shadow of its former self when evacuated.

The battalion was moved by ship to Imbros, a staging post for the army on a small island to the west of the Gallipoli peninsular. "The first impressions of Imbros were far from pleasant. During the night a strong gale arose and practically all the tents being pitched on rocky ground which gave pegs no grip, came down on their wretched occupants. To make matters worse our kit had gone astray, and we had nothing but the clothes we stood up in and one blanket." Brigadier Erskine took over the brigade on boxing day, and 200 other ranks arrived from the divisional depot. The soldiers started low level training, including gentle walking and playing on the two football pitches.

Details of the battalion's actions during the campaign were lost to memory as the battalion war diary was lost at Sea during the evacuation. 12 of the soldiers killed were listed from Walsall, 4 were married. Such news was a shock for the home front, as were wounded soldiers returning home via the Regimental Depot in Lichfield. On the 28th January 1916 the battalion sailed on HMT Oriana to Alexandria, arriving on the 2nd February and given passes to explore the suburbs of the city.

On 19th February, the battalion took over the defences (Number 3 Section Canal Defences) on the Suez Canal where they would remain until the summer of 1916. The routine of the garrison posting was difficult, especially as many of the most experienced non-commissioned officers had been killed in the campaign, and replacements has little experience. It was a hard time for the battalion. Thomas Craddock was now a Lance Corporal and took his share of the responsibility on this garrison duty. For those who had survived the campaign in Gallipoli, it was with mixed emotions they were away from the front line. The battalion continued to train, including with artillery of the 5th Brigade Royal Field Artillery at Sidi Bishr. The battalion was also joined by two horses, Peter the Commanding Officer's horse who survived until September 1918, and Sover, the Adjutant's who would also survive until June 1918. In early March the battalion lost three officers and 32 other ranks to form the Brigade machine gun company. The battalion were issued four Vickers guns to replace the two lost Lewis guns from the campaign. The battalion also spent 36 days building new defences east of the canal as the original defences were on the west bank and these were deemed as ineffective.

On June the 28th 1916, 25 Officer and 628 other ranks left Ballah on the Suez Canal. On 29th June the battalion embarked on HMS Mineewaska at Alexandria, (they shared the ship with the 6th Lincolnshire Regiment). The ship sailed for Marseilles on July the 2nd, where they landed on 7th July. They then travelled by train with the rest of the 11th Division to the Western Front.

Chapter 4
Home Front

As the battalion embarked from Imbros to travel to Sidi Bashir in Egypt on 28th January 1916, the situation on the home front was very difficult with the German U-boat campaign on the increase, a real threat of invasion and for the first time bombing of civilian targets from the air, in the shape of Zeppelin raids. These changes made living on the home front hard for Thomas' family, who were directly impacted in many ways.

In Walsall, James continued to work in the leather industry with his oldest son Joseph, who in 1916 was 41 and therefore avoided conscription. Thomas' Sarah (45), Eliza (43) and Louisa (31) were married with their own families living in the Butts, and his mother Mary lives with his sister Ellan (36), Mary (26) and brother Robert (24). Robert was applying to join the Royal Navy Reserve, and despite being in a key industry, was keen to serve his country in this role. Ellan had a daughter Elizabeth, (Cissi), who lived in their home, and remembered the experience of war time Britain vividly.[1] Thomas' brother James Esra (38) had joined the 1st Battalion Loyal North Lancashire Regiment at the outbreak of war and was in France. His younger brother Frank William was 27 and had joined the 3rd Battalion of the South Staffordshire Regiment, but they were not posted overseas, having been based in Sunderland and then Newcastle as part of Tyneside Garrison.

With a severe shortage of skilled workers, industry redesigned work so that it could be done by unskilled men and women meaning that war-related industries grew rapidly. Walsall was no exception, with huge increases in mining and in work in the metal and leather works around the town. All of

---

[1] It is Cicci Maon who recorded her experiences later in life and left an oral record.

Mary's daughter now worked full time jobs as well as looking after their children. Cissi's father Albert was 54, and a jewel maker who worked in Walsall doing critical war work for long hours. He was also a union man, who collected the union fees and negotiated with employers. The prime minister Lloyd George cut a deal with the trades unions, they approved the dilution of labour (since it would be temporary) and threw their organizations into the war effort, but Albert kept an eye on the impact of this in his role.

On 4 February 1915, Germany declared a war zone around Britain, within which merchant ships were sunk without warning. This unrestricted submarine warfare angered neutral countries, especially the United States. The tactic was abandoned on 1 September 1915, following the loss of American lives in the torpedoed liners Lusitania and Arabic. However, despite this warfare Britian had a huge industrial might and strong farming sector, so rationing and restrictions were not needed at this point. When the US joined the war, U-Boats increased again between February and April 1917, U-boats sank more than 500 merchant ships. In the second half of April, an average of 13 ships were sunk each day. This meant that the British Government had no choice but to bring in restrictions.

Voluntary rationing was introduced in February 1917 with bread being subsidised from September that year. Compulsory rationing was introduced in stages between December 1917 and February 1918 as Britain's supply of wheat decreased to just six weeks' consumption. To help the process, ration books were introduced in July 1918 for butter, margarine, lard, meat, and sugar. Unlike most of Europe, bread was not rationed but rationing remained in some form until 1921.

At home, Cissi remembered the increase in animals in the garden during the war, with a pig, chickens and ducks, as well as a goat. Ellan continued to work hard cleaning, having to get up early each day at 5am, but Cissi was always up first with a cup of tea for her. As soon as her mom left the house, from the introduction of rationing in 1918 Cissi was left at the age of 8 in the line at Coopers shop in Stafford Street with the ration book waiting for food. Mary would finish work at 9am, take over in the queue, and Cici would then run off to school. Cissi attended the girls school on the Butts, and used to enjoy helping Mr Venables the care taker to stoke the coal fire for the school's heating system. When she got home, her mother would have made stew from the mutton and dripping on the ration book, and mixed it with fresh vegetables from the garden. There was only fresh food, and no tins were available at this time. After eating, Cissi would run out to the garden and wash the pots outside, just next to the outside toilet and amongst the animals.

Even with the war, Cissi enjoyed being a young girl. Her fondest memory was being allowed to travel to Sutton Park with her friends. On her return journey, she was accused of having her feet on the seat of the tram by a conductor. Later that night a Police Officer came round to question her mother about the incident, and Cissi hid in the garden 'doing the washing up!'

The biggest change to the morale of the local population in Walsall, was the first Zeppelin raid on the town itself.[2] A fleet of nine aircraft bombed the Midlands on the night of 31st January 1916 killing 60 people. Bombs landed on Wednesbury, Walsall, Tipton and Bilston, where 35 people across the area died.

---

[2] The following story is largely taken from news paper reports from the day.

The first attack was by Zeppelin L.21, which had mistaken the black country and the canals below for the docks of Liverpool, which were its original target. The airships had the ability to hover above a target, and by doing so were very accurate in their bombing. Many of the casualties were caused when the airship dropped the first bomb, people ran outside causing a flash of light, which led to repeat bombs being dropped on the same location. *Kapitanleutnant* Max Dietrich of the Imperial German Navy commanded the air ship and was lost after nine hours of trying to find his target. The Black Country has no blackout enforced, and the lights reflected on the many waterways made it look like the docks. The airship was a new 'Q Type' airship over 585ft in length and a crew of 17 airmen.

The attack started in Tipton at 8pm with three high explosive bombs dropped on Waterloo Street and Union Street by the bomb aimer *Leutnant zur See* Christian Von Nathusius. This was quickly followed by three incendiary bombs on Bloomfield Road and Barnfield Road. In Union Street two houses were demolished and others damaged, the gas main was set alight. Fourteen Tipton people were killed, five men, five women and four children, this included three generations of one family killed. The main gas main under the street was set alight. The areas was between two canals making it look like a dock area, which is what was later written in the airships report.

Thomas Morris, a witness at the Tipton Coroner's Inquest, spoke of the harrowing story. He had gone to the cinema, the Tivoli in Owen Street, when he heard the bombs. His wife had taken the children to her mother's. When he reached her house in Union Street it was completely demolished, inside he found five bodies, his wife, Sarah Jane Morris, two of his children, Nellie Morris, aged eight and Martin Morris aged 11, along with his mother and father-in-law.

From Tipton, the Zeppelin moved to Lower Bradley following the Great Western railway line, dropping three incendiary bombs on the Bloomfield Brickworks and then five high explosive bombs on Bradley Pumping Station and killing a young couple, Maud and William Fellows, on the bank of the Wolverhampton Union Canal. Their death is commemorated by a plaque on the wall of the Bradley pumping station, which still exists today. The bomber then moved to attack Wednesbury at 8.15pm, killing 14 people, four men, six women and four children, in the area of King Street, near the Crown Tube works. Bombs also fell at the back of the Crown and Cushion Inn in High Bullen, and Brunswick Park Road.

At about 8.15pm, Mrs Smith of 14 King Street heard an alarming loud bang. She ran out of the house to see what was happening, leaving in the house her husband, her daughter Nelly aged 13, her son Thomas aged 11, and her daughter Ina aged seven, when she returned, they had all disappeared. The bodies of Joseph, Nelly and Thomas were found later that night in the ruins of number 13 King Street which suffered a direct hit by a bomb. The fate of little Ina aged seven was even more tragic. Her body was not found until the next morning. It had been blown onto the roof of the James Russell Works by the explosion.

After leaving Wednesbury Dietrich headed north for Walsall, the first bomb landed on Wednesbury Road Congregational Church, on the corner of Wednesbury Road and Glebe Street. A preparation class from the local primary school was working in the church parlour and miraculously no one was killed, though a man walking outside had the top of his head blown off. The Zeppelins then flew over the centre of Walsall. Bombs landed in the grounds of the General Hospital, and Montrath Street.

The last bomb landed right in the town centre, outside the Science and Art Institute in Bradford Place. This bomb claimed three lives including the best-known Zeppelin victim, 55 year old Mary Julia Slater, the Lady Mayoress of Walsall. She was a passenger on the number 16 tram. She suffered severe wounds, was taken to hospital and died several weeks later on Sunday, February 20, 1916. The Walsall Cenotaph now stands on the spot where the bomb landed.

This first part of the raid by L.21 killed 35 people and injured 29. However, the raid had not yet finished with Zeppelin L.19 again bombing the Black Country after midnight, but was also the only airship to not return from the raid. Thought the press claimed there was no panic, this is certainly an exaggeration with tens of thousands of people hearing the bombs and seeing the Zepelin in flight. The fires could be seen from miles around, and the impact had caused trams to stop running and blackouts to be enforced. L.19 was commanded by *kapitanleutnant* Odo Loewe who was a veteran of three earlier raids.

L.19 first bombed Burton-on-Trent and then travelled south as far as Kidderminster. After Midnight the Zeppelin had turned north and dropped a bomb on the Monway Works in Wednesbury, and then a further five high explosive bombs on the Ocker Hill Colliery and a further seventeen bombs on Dudley itself. From here he could see the burning gas mains in Tipton and dropped eleven high explosive bombs on the area. One bomb hit the roof of the Bush Inn, bounced off and exploded in front, blowing out the door and smashing the windows. The clock in the pub was hit by shrapnel and stopped on the impact at twenty past midnight. One man, William Henry Haycock, age 50, was killed at 53 Bescot Street, Pelfrey.

Across much of England the blackout was not enforced, and where it was, old gas lights had to be put out by hand, with a person with a long pole. Such actions took a long time and were very ineffective. However, the results of these raids would lead to a wider enforcement of the blackout, with the subsequent impact on life at home. The physical damage was there for all to see in the town, especially the impact on pubs and churches which were used by all. The casualties of civilians were a huge shock to the people across the Midlands and Black Country, but closest to home were the six people killed in Walsall:

Charles Cope Age 34
Frank Thomas Linney Age 36
Thomas Merrylees Age 28
Mary Julia Slater Age 55
John Thomas Powell Age 59
William Henry Haycock Age 50

A side note to the raid was that L.19, after crossing the English coat in Norfolk at 5.25am had engine trouble. Combined with navigation issues, this led to the airship ditching in the North Sea. The crew survived and were seen by a British fishing trawler King Stephen, who refused to pick up the German crew fearing they would be taken over by the soldiers and forced to go to Germany. The Zeppelin later sunk with all hands lost.

James and Mary were stunned by the turn of event, and the whole family was in a stake of shock that such actions could take place so close to home. The bombs had landed less than a mile from their home, and it was perceived that the German targets could have been the war factories where many of the ladies in the family now worked. The impact of the Zeppelin attacks on the battalion overseas was huge, soldiers were incredulous that such attacks could be made on the home front against the civilian population. Morale in the battalion suffered accordingly, with many questioning when they would be able to fight the real enemy, the Germans.

Chapter 5

France 1916

By July 1916, the stalemate of trench warfare had been ongoing for 18 months. The British offensive at the Battle of Loos had failed with a loss of 50,000 men, and the Somme offensive in July 1916 had been disastrous for the new Kitchener Army, with 56,000 casualties on the first day alone. It was in this context that on 18th July, the 7th (Service) Battalion South Staffordshire Regiment joined the line on the Western Front.

The battalion took over a stretch of the front line known as 'H Sector' from 9th Battalion King's Royal Rifle Corps. The Strength of the battalion had increased with replacements to 39 officers and 990 other ranks in four rifle companies. At this time, as is the routine in battalion life, five officers and 67 other ranks were away on courses. The situation on the Western Front was difficult, with a major British offensive taking place on the 1st July, seeing the Kitcher Army suffer terrible losses. On the first day alone, the British Army suffered 57,470 casualties including 19,240 killed. Over the next six months, over a million men across both sides would be killed and wounded, a scale of loss which is shocking to comprehend.

On July 24th the first casualty in the battalion was 34 year old Private Joseph Davies of Brockmore, Staffordshire, who was killed on the wiring party at night. Wiring parties were groups of soldiers who were sent out into no man's land to adjust and repair the barbed wire in front of the trenches.

The battalion was stationed in Arras which was part of the 3rd Army, it was considered to by a gentler part of the front for a new battalion. The billets in the rear areas were basic, with mud walls and much poverty, however the

French civilians were still living there despite the enemy fire. Behind the trenches, when in reserve, the battalion conducted training in route marches to harden feet after Egypt, and also a lot of training in anti-gas drills. The 33rd Brigade trench mortar battery formed, with one officer and 31 other ranks posted there to form this unit. An abiding memory of this sector were the beautiful flowers in the support trenches, including red, white and blue poppies, daises and cornflowers. Another memory was of Captain Bailey, who had a penchant for killing rats, but was seen as a greater threat that the Germans!

At the end of July, the Battalion Adjutant wrote in the war diary a summary of their first month on the trench line:

> *"A month of many experiences and hard work, which the battalion has stood with continuous route marches on hard surfaces was very trying, but the men took it extremely well in spite of the bad boots and leather feel. The keenness shown in the trenches, after the long spell of inactivity, is most marked. The numerous fatigues, which occupation of trenches demands, patrolling, observing and sniping, have all been diligently carried on. No doubt the 'push' on our night has inspired all ranks, and then so the moral is exceptionally good, considering that many officers and men are new to trench conditions, close proximity to the enemy, The weather has been kind with little rain having fallen."*

Two further soldiers were killed in July, Private Charles Twigg of Small Health Birmingham, and Private Fredd Lappage. Such losses were the routine of trench warfare, whether through shell fire, snipers, or just accidents. In August, William Bills of Wednesbury was killed. By September the battalion had got used to life on the Western Front, with its routine of long periods of quiet, and short intense periods of combat. The constant trickle of replacements brought the battalion up to strength, and old soldiers who had served in Gallipoli in 1915 were getting fewer. Thomas, now a corporal was an old soldier, commanding much respect in A Company. He had been away from home for 18 months, and there was no end in sight to this terrible warfare.

On 6th September, the battalion took up defensive positions on the Somme within the support line of the trenches at Aucheux wood. As they marched in to billets, the battalion's soldiers looked in good condition compared to the other units they took over from. On the 4th September the battalion moved into the line. All around was the little of war, with no sign of the villages marked on the map. A and B Company held the front, A Company was based on the left flank covering the battalion boundary and the support line of the Brigade. D Company in the support 'X Line' and C Company in reserve. At one time this had been the German front line. Captain Worcester of A company was killed by a sniper, he has been with the battalion since Gallipoli., then the next day Captain Christian by a shell near A Company HQ, he was the battalion intelligence officer.

The Battalion joined 32nd Brigade temporarily and although described as a quiet period, they received heavy shelling, killing three soldiers and wounding eleven. A clearing party was sent forward to collect materials and pushed forward several saps (small trenches). Whilst doing this work, Captain Harold Worcester, aged 22 from Bristol was killed along with Privates Stein and Hyardse being wounded.

The difficult defensive work continued, with digging and clearance at night, led by work parties across the flanks and no man's land, a difficult task, and very dangerous. The plan was to push saps into no man's land and form a new front line closer to the German positions. On the night of 11th September, the Germans launched tear gas shells at the Royal Field Artillery battery in the support positions but hitting the battalion also. One high explosive shell landed in a trench and killed Captain Edward Christian a 21 year old officer from the Isle of Mann. Despite these difficulties and terrible conditions, the digging of another sap, was completed by 5am. The next day the battalion were relieved by the 6th Battalion, the Border Regiment, and moved to the reserve billets at Bouzincourt. Here, Brigadier Clating, the Brigade Commander, expressed his great pleasure at the excellent work done in 'Stafford Trench' forming a new front line.

Throughout the rest of the month the routine of the battalion continued on the Somme, at Thiepval Wood and Beaumont Hamal. During this time 60 soldiers were killed, including two captains, two lieutenants, two sergeants and three junior NCOs. This was a very active part of the front, continuing from the major offensive in July, now into large skirmish actions, counterattacks and large scale shelling. During 27th September Reverent Wilkes endeared himself to the battalion, he walked forward and brought several wounded back in. He was awarded the Military Medal for these actions.

The morning of 28th September passed quietly considering but the trenches were constantly shelled with shrapnel and high explosive shells. In the afternoon the battalion stood to an attack being reported coming from Stuff Redoubt. One company was moved into Schwaber Trench to relieve congestion in the front line, casualties being heavy. The night passed quietly, except the constant shelling.

The battalion were on the move again moving to Beaucourt marching to Hedauville on the 28th September a distance of six miles, where they entrained at Acheux for Candas a further 30 kilometres. After training in the rear areas, on the 9th December the battalion marches towards the river Ancre, taking up billets in the rear area at Domleger, then Maison-Rolland by the 6th November. Brigadier Ersuime Commander of the 33rd Infantry Brigade inspected the battalion and complemented them on the way they acted in recent operations. For the next month, the battalion trained in billets, conducting route marches, bombing training and attacks in both trenches and the open. Specialist training was provided to Lewis gunners, bombers, signallers and snipers.

During the month, 10 officers and 170 other ranks joined the battalion, of which half had previously served in the battalion in Egypt or Gallipoli and were returning from injury or courses. On 7th October the Corps Commander, Lieutenant General Jacobs inspected the battalion and paid further complements. On 21st October, four Military Medals were awarded to LCpl R Jodd and Privates Beston, Hendley and Guest. By November the battalion had increased its strength to 39 Officers and 880 other ranks.

On 20th November, after six weeks of training and reorganisation the battalion were on the move again to the front. They took over the from the 6th Battalion Yorkshire and Lancashire Regiment at Beaucourt. During the first night of occupation five men were killed and seven wounded by the heavy shell fire, including the Regimental Medical Officer Capture Harpur who was wounded. The incessant shelling would continue throughout the week with two further deaths and sixteen wounded on the second night in the line, and four further wounded the third night. These casualties showed the large number of new soldiers in the battalion, who had not learned the basic drills of remaining low and in cover in the trenches, but also many were simply bad luck. Many were experienced which included Private Harry Bellfield age 21 from Wolverhampton who had been awarded the Military Medal in Gallipoli and Lance Corporal Fred Sanders from Handsworth in Birmingham who was 31. By 29th November, when the battalion was relieved by the 6th Battalion, The Yorkshire Regiment, and 32nd Brigade, they had suffered over 70 casualties with 33 soldiers killed.

The Commanding Officer, Lieutenant Colonel Stikham wrote of this last battle of 1916:

> *The last ten days have been the most trying experience by the battalion. The men were continuously exposed to accurate shell fire, from which there was no adequate cover, and therefore there was a constant drain of casualties. Excellent work was done by the following who were all killed; Sgt Birch, Cpl Bleasdale, Cpl Woodhouse, Sgt Tuek and Pte Blunsdell. It must be recorded that despite of these losses; the morale of the battalion was never better.*

At this time the second in command wrote that the greatest challenge was the weather, with an extreme cold spell making life in the trenches very hard. On Christmas day the battalion was sent up the line to the same sector, it was a weirdly silent day, with the British artillery firing only short bursts. On boxing day, the artillery returned to normal. The quality of replacement soldiers was becoming worse, with soldiers only getting 12 weeks training in England. A Brigade school was formed behind the line to conduct further training.

Since their arrival in France, the battalion had lost 121 soldiers and many more were wounded. Four officers had been killed, including Captain Harold

Worcester and Captain Edward Christian as well as four sergeants and nineteen junior NCOs. Every town across the United Kingdom was informed of men from their homes being killed and Walsall was no exception, with men across the army coming from the town. Of the 7th Battalion, young soldiers such as Private Frank Barnett, son of Mary Ann Barnett, of 26, Haskell Street, Walsall, were killed and Mary Ann had to suffer the loss of such a young man in the prime of his life. Other were fathers, such as Private Harry Collins from Bilston, who at age 46 was married to Alice, who now had to survive on the limited war payout she was given. Every man killed had a story and was a son, husband or father. This scale of loss is terrible to think of.

42

Chapter 6
1917

1917 began with the battalion receiving fire from a known 5.9-inch German gun across no man's land, but no casualties were reported. On 2nd January, the battalion were relieved by the 9th Sherwood Foresters and moved rest billets where they received sixty-nine other ranks from the 9th Infantry Depot. The commanding officer Lieutenant Colonel Seckham received notice in the new year's honours list that he was awarded a Distinguished Service Order for leadership. With the difficult weather, there was an increase in non-battle casualties even in billets, with twenty-nine cases of scabies moved to hospital in a week behind the lines. The battalion returned to the front line again on 9th January, with the routine of trench life continuing. The artillery on the front carried on at a high tempo, as did aggressive patrolling by the battalion, on the 9th January, Private Philios and LCpl Willcox of A Company wounded, the first of the year. On most days there were casualties, some days worse than others. On 11th January, four soldiers were killed and five wounded.

On 18th January, the battalion went into billets again, moving from Ancre where they were relieved by the Naval Division. More awards from the combat of late 1916 were announced, with Lieutenant Colonel Seckham, Major Ashcroft and Sergeant Allchin all receiving Mentions in Despatches. This time the battalion moved well behind the lines, to a permanent rest area at Cramont. Three days were spent with individual preparation and rest, followed by a week of intense physical and musket training. On 31st January, General Officer Commanding 11th Division inspected the battalion and commented on their excellent turn out. Snow was on the ground and the battalion was now back up to full strength with 42 officers and 969 other ranks.

The training continued to the 13h February, but was not without incident. On 12th February, 2nd Lieutenant West was killed in a hand grenade incident, with three soldiers wounded. From 13th February the battalion marched towards a new position on the Western Front with 33rd Infantry Brigade. Each day the battalion marched around 15 miles, but large numbers of soldiers fell out. The adjutant commented that the main causes were inferior boots and tender feet due to prolonged frost. Also, it was added that marching order was now too heavy with leather jerkins added for winter. It is interesting to see the maturity of this view, and the blame was not given to any inefficiency or unfitness of the men. After three days of marching, the brigade joined the rear lines and stared construction details on a strategic railway. Nine hours a day were spent on this physical labour which was being constructed with a Canadian railway battalion to create a new supply line to the front line. The front line had been moved forwards as the German forces after the campaign on the Somme had moved back to the Hindenburg line.

On 8th March, it was announced that Captain Ashcroft was to be appointed temporary Major and Second in Command and a new commander of 33rd Infantry Brigade was appointed, Brigadier General H R Davies. On 24th March the Brigade moved again to the XVIII Corps area under the command of Lieutenant General Maxse. The battalion had worked hard behind the lines for this month period and enjoyed being away from the front and the difficult fighting conditions. Now in another permanent rest camp at Sarton, the battalion went into another intensive training period, starting at platoon level and building up to specialist training in wood fighting and open warfare. On 9th April, it was announced that the spring offensive had started, and the battalion was ordered to be ready to move to the front if needed. This was later to be known as the Battle of Arras.

Training continued for the rest of the month, with the battalion marching out on 21st April to the front line at Boursies, on the Cambrai – Bapaume Road. On the 24th, the battalion took over as the sector night battalion from 1st Australian Infantry Brigade, on the same day Major General Richie was wounded and command of the 11th Division was passed to Brigadier Davies. The line taken over was not heavily entrenched or provided with dug outs and cover as the battalion had previously known. However, also was absent of the 'semi open warfare' that Corps HQ had told them was the case during the last week. The line was a series of small positions, and in not all cases well sited. Each man has a small firing step, but there is no wire to the front. Communication to the front posts by day was impossible, with the enemy 1500 yards away with open arcs of fire over the positions. There was heavy shelling throughout the sector. During the first night the battalion lost 2nd Lieutenant Tinkler and Private Morris killed, with Private Evans wounded. The battalion held the line until 30th April, when the 5th Dorset Regiment of 34th Brigade conducted a relief in place. The battalion moved to the support position at Beaumetz, holding the flanks of the divisional sector.

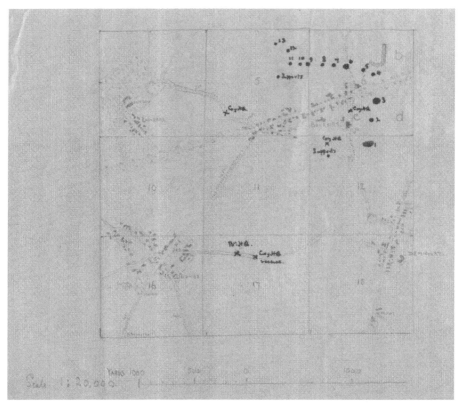

Image 4: Operations May 1917 (Battalion War Diary)

The battalion remained in the support line for the first week of May, on the 6th May relieved the 6th West Yorkshire Regiment in front of Demicourt on the front line. The position had no immediate support line to the rear but had a sunken road in which two of the company headquarters' were located. The position overall was a series of strong points, rather than a continuous line. A Company took the three right hand positions. The companies sent patrols forward and found no man's land to be full of small trenches and posts which had been abandoned, increasing the threat of enemy infiltration.

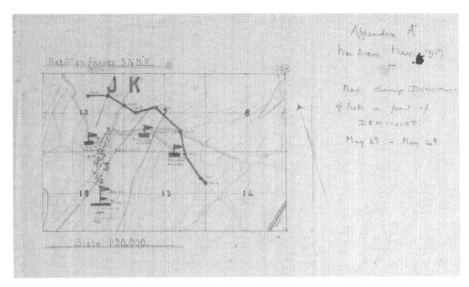

Image 5: Operations 6th May 1917 (Battalion War Diary)

On the 10th May a patrol of A Company found an enemy party in no man's land, however both the Germans and the company patrols did not engage and pulled back to their own lines. Artillery and machine gun fire was very active across the front over this period. On the 14th May, the battalion was relieved by the Poachers Battalion of the Oxford Poachers light Infantry. The battalion pulled back again to a rest area in the vicinity of Carndy.

The Battle of Arras was coming to an end, and although considerable gains had been made at the start of the battle, by the end of the battle, the British had suffered over 150,000 casualties. In the wider context of the front the battle had very little impact on the strategic situation and did not achieve a breakout. On the 14th May 1917 the battalion was relieved from the line and moved to Belgian Town of Fletre for planning of Messines – Wytschaete offensive.

Orders were received on the 15th May that the battalion, as part of the 11th Division, was to join 2nd Army, under General Plumber, for a general offensive near Messines. Brigadier General A C Daily took over command of the 33rd Infantry Brigade and on the 18th May, the battalion moved by train to Boulogne, then Calais and after 15 hours were in a rear area camp at Fletre. The Commander of the 5th Army which the battalion left sent a note to thank the battalion for its service as part of the army. On 24th May, Regimental Sergeant Major Griffiths and five other members of the battalion were mentioned in despatches by Field Marshall Sir Douglas Haig.

For the remainder of May and up to 6th June, the battalion trained in the rear areas but received their orders for the coming offensive. The 33rd Infantry Brigade had the role of exploiting any success made by the 17th Infantry Division as part of IX Corps during the attack on the Wytschaete-Messines Ridge, the brigade moto for the attack was bullet – bayonet – bullet, to get in close to the enemy. 33rd Infantry Brigade was attached to 16th (Irish) Division to attack the Wtschaete Ridge, and a mile beyond. 2nd ANZAC Corps was on the right, and X Corps to the left. The attack was made into dead ground, with only aerial observation made before the assault.

The lead battalions for the assault would be the 6th Lincolnshire Regiment, 9th Sherwood Foresters and 6th Border Regiment, with the 7th South Staffordshire Regiment in immediate support. On 6th June the battalion moved to the form up positions with zero hour (the start of the attack) set for 03:10 the following day.

At 01:05 the orders changed to include two companies of the 7th South Staffordshire Regiment, to be attached to the 6th Lincolnshire Regiment on the initial assault. At 02:56, the battalion moved into its deployment formation for the attack, on the left was one company from 6th Lincolnshire, the D Company in the centre and A Company on the right. The men were exhausted having marched for four hours already in full equipment. At 3.10pm they were ready to assault over the Mauve line. The Borderers and Lincolnshire did not make the front line in time, so the 7th South Staffordshire Regiment advanced alone with the 6th Lincolns, two companies in the lead, A and D. B and C Companies in support lost touch with the lead elements. A and D Company separated on the advance, with much confusion; mines had been exploded, heavy artillery used across the frontage, and burning oil drums were used to light up enemy trenches and burn the enemy out.

B and C Company lost touch with Battalion HQ and waited at Romens Farm, which was not reached until 3.50am. The main body had advanced on to the main objectives under heavy artillery fire. There were few landmarks and then men were exhausted; D company found itself isolated on reaching the Mauve Line, but the Officer Commanding pushed on to find 13th Brigade (Australian Army) on this right flank and 57th Brigade on his left, continuing the advance for the whole brigade onto Odour Trench the enemy front line, which the company cleared of the enemy taking 15 prisoners. D Company then proceeded to clear the dug outs.

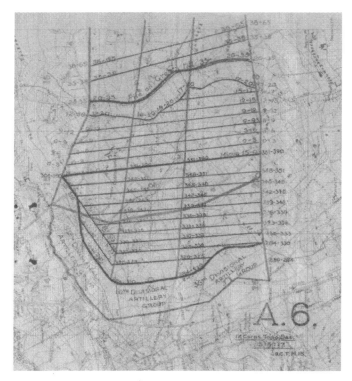

Image 6: Operations 6th May 1917 (Battalion War Diary)

Meanwhile A Company also lost direction, and coming through a heavy barrage crossed the Mauve Line under heavy fire from enemy dug outs. The company charged forward and bombed the enemy positions, taking five prisoners. With little support, the company pulled back to the battalion headquarters at Mahieu Farm.

Early the next morning, the enemy were seen massing on the front, and patrols were ordered forward to find out what was happening. They were pinned down by snipers. At 10:45, the enemy started shelling the battalion headquarters and the Commanding Officer Lieutenant Colonel Seckham was wounded, and Captain Morris assumed command. At 11:30 Major Ashcroft had moved forward and took over command. The battalion with A and D

Companies forward then dug in. The next day, the 10th June, the battalion was heavily shelled as neighbouring units took up the offensive.

> *The loss of Colonel Seckham was very deeply felt throughout the battalion, which thoroughly understood how much of its success was due to his personal efforts. Both in Gallipoli and France, his untiring energy combined with a genial disposition had made him deeply loved. Throughout his command, the battalion never suffered a reverse. He found the battalion a wreck of its former self and left it as a fine a fighting unit as anyone could desire.*

On the 11th June, the battalion was pulled back into reserve near Spy Farm. Over the period of fighting between the 7th and 10th June, the battalion lost 26 soldiers and 86 were wounded, including the commanding officer. Again, the battalion was moved to Clare Camp near Dranoutre, and returned to XVIII Corps and 5th Army, near Ypres. The battalion moved again to billets at La Commune, where they would train in the rear areas. During this camp they were allowed swimming, football and rest.

On 12th June a special order of the day was issued by GOC 2nd Army:

> *The GOC 2nd Army has personally expressed his great appreciation of the good work done by the troops of the 11th Division in the recent battle. He wishes to add his own thanks to all ranks of the Division for what they have done.*

> *The 11th Division artillery and ammunition column, the 68th Field Coy RE, the 32nd, 33rd and 34th Companies Machine Gun Corps, the 33rd*

Infantry Brigade and certain forces of the Field Ambulances were able to take part in the battle and fully upheld their reputation.

Other units of the Division by the hard work done, both before and during the battle work often carried our under fire, contributed materially to the victory.

On 15th July the battalion were again forward in the front line, taking over trenches from the 4/5th Black Watch about a mile north of Ypres. The battalion had the role of holding and improving the line for the preparation for the Paschaendale Ridge attack. Which was to form part of the third battle of Ypres. The 33rd Brigade came under the command of 51st Highland Division. During the relief in place Private Cobley was wounded. The next morning the enemy sent over a large number of gas shells, causing much irritation to the soldiers' eyes, although no casualties. Over the following week, the heavy artillery fire caused a constant flow of casualties, on the 17th July one soldier was killed and nine wounded, on the 18th July three soldiers were killed and twelve wounded. The 19th July saw two soldiers being killed and fourteen wounded, on the 20th three were wounded and on both the 21st and 22nd five were wounded, including Regimental Sergeant Major Purchas. At 11:00 on 22nd July, the battalion was relieved by the 6th Border Regiment, and Lieutenant Colonel W H Carter arrived to take over command. However, during the handover, a gas attack is launched, and there was a considerable delay.

The story of Harry Carter is as incredible as many throughout this war, a man who would promote from Private to Brigadier. Harry joined the army on 20th December 1899 having served in the Boar War and promoted to Lance Corporal as part of the 2nd Battalion, the South Staffordshire Regiment. He was commissioned 2nd Lieutenant in the field on 4 January 1915. In the next three years, following rapid promotion, he proved himself to be a superb and highly regarded infantry officer, showing bravery and leadership qualities during some of the heaviest fighting on the Western Front. On 19th July 1917 Harry Carter, aged 38, was appointed Acting Lieutenant Colonel as the Commanding Officer of the 7th South Staffordshire Regiment, in 33 Brigade, 11th (Northern) Division. This was an appointment he was to hold for the rest of the war.

54

Chapter 7

Passchendaele

For the next week heavy shelling continued along the support line causing numerous casualties in the battalion. Patrols were sent out to the flanks, and small operations took place. The battle was part of the right sub-sector of the 51st Division, from Finch Street on the right, to Clark Street on the left. The battalion had two forward companies with two support companies, the forward companies moved forward each night to occupy strong points.

On 27th July, Royal Flying Corps observers saw the German lines retreating, later that day orders were given, with 50 minutes notice for the battalion to advance and occupy the enemy positions. The advance on zero hour was hap hazard with some battalions making the timeline, and others not. During this attack Private Barrett 17114 took part in actions for which he would later be awarded a Victoria Cross. Private Barratt was acting as a scout to one of the patrols consisting of one officer and 25 men, send forward to locate enemy positions. Under sniper and machine gun fire, we moved forward and killed six enemy and captured some documents. The enemy tried to outflank the patrol, and Private Barratt volunteered to stay behind whilst the patrol crawled back. He stayed in place, killing many of the enemy and allowed the patrol to escape. Whilst moving back to line, he was instantly killed by a shell.

On 28th July, the battalion was relieved by the 19th Kings Royal Rifle Corps and pulled back from the line. Out of the line the battalion spent the 1st of August bathing and conducting show parades ready for ceremonial drill. The effective strength of the battalion had dropped to 717 soldiers and 34 officers. During a parade on 6th August four soldiers received the Military Medal, Sergeant Powell, Lance Sergeant Price, Lance Corporal Harrison and Private

Perkins. Planning now took place for a further operation which was to start on 16th August. This was what was to become the battle of the Battle of Langemarck (16–18 August 1917), part of the third battle of Ypres.

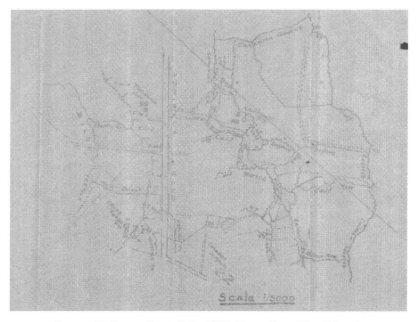

Image 7: Operations July 1917 (Battalion War Diary)

At 05:30 on 16th August the battalion moved into the Caledonia Reserve Trenches in preparation for any Counterattack, with A Company forward right, and B company forward left. C and D company formed the immediate reserve. At 07:00 the battalion moved forward in section fire and manoeuvre through no man's land, but by 08:15 B company became lost, and A C and D company dug in under a heavy barrage of enemy fire. At 10:20 it was reported that enemy were massing at Poelcapelle, and counterattacks during the afternoon forced the British back to their starting positions in many areas. Attacks continued over the next two days, utilising creeping barrages, smoke and even, on the 19th, a combined arms assault with tanks. On the morning of the 20th, the battalion was relieved by the 6th Lincolnshire Regiment, having suffered two officers and 87 other ranks killed during the action.

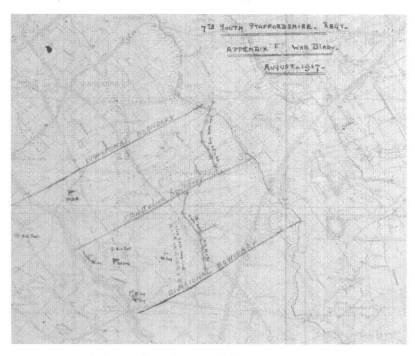

Image 8: Operations August 1917 (Battalion War Diary)

The next three days were spent in the rear, mainly used to move ammunition to the line. On the night of the 22nd August the Commanding Officer and Adjutant slept in the open in two large water tanks. A German shell landed between them, causing no damage. With little rest, the battalion relieved the 6th Border Regiment on 24th August, moving back to the forward trenches. However, this time the battalion were only in position for three days, suffering seven casualties. On 29th August the battalion and whole 11th Division were relieved by the 51st Division and moved to the rear areas.

The following quote is during the relief, written by a soldier looking back in 1919:

> *You are standing in a muddy trench on a pitch-dark night, waiting for the friendly sound of the relief coming up the communication trench, and picturing yourself in a comfy dug-out further to the rear. The intensity of the darkness is only relieved at intervals by the Boche white lights, which as they flicker out, leave you in greater darkness that ever. Suddenly there is a sound as of the top taken off a syphon, followed by a sharp 'phut'. The Boche is using gas-shells, and you feel irritation in the nose, and a burning down the back of your throat. "Box respirators on" is passed down, but you are already in position. If you were in the dark now you are practically blind. Phut – phut – phut all round you; the place is simply being deluged with the beastly stuff and you know it will not clear away for hours.*

September started with the battalion back in the rear areas and training, receiving 85 other ranks in a first draft, then 133 in a second and a third of 26, bringing the battalion up to strength again with 27 officers and 918 other ranks in total. Training was focused on dealing with 'Pill Boxes' of rectangular concrete type, but also three days were given over to a brigade sports competition, which included football, boxing and cross country running. On 12th September, seven soldiers were awarded the Military Medal for the actions at Ypres; Sergeant Deighton, Sergeant Pugh, Corporal Wilkinson, Lance Corporal Taylor, Private Martin, Private Andrews and Private Butterick. Captain Charlton was awarded the Military Cross, and Lance Corporal Blewitt the Distinguished Conduct Medal. After a month in camp, on 3rd October the battalion move to Canal Bank, reliving the 6th Battalion, the Yorkshire Regiment.

On 3rd October 1917, the 7th Battalion South Staffordshire Regiment took part in the battle of Broodseinde and capture of Poelkapelle, in what is known as the Battle of Passchendaele. The battle lasted for four days and the battalion left the line on 8th October having suffered about 120 casualties. The attack aimed to complete the capture of the Gheluvelt Plateau by the occupation of Broodseinde Ridge and Gravenstafel Spur. This would protect the southern flank of the British line and permit attacks on Passchendaele Ridge to the north-east.

The offensive was planned by both the British second and fifth armies, to attack the positions of the 4th German Army. The attack was planned to use bite and hold tactics, with objectives limited to what could be held against German counterattacks. This was in much the same way as the tactics used during the offensive in August that the battalion had been involved in. Divisions attacked on narrower fronts and troops advanced no more than 1,500 yards into the German defence zone, before consolidating their position. The German defenders on the plateau had launches over twenty Counterattacks during the last month, but these had been costly failures by them. When the Germans counter-attacked, they encountered a reciprocal defence-in-depth, protected by a mass of artillery, and suffered many casualties to little effect.

October 1st and 2nd were spent being issued battle equipment for the offensive to come. The battle area was famous for its liquid mud, and the offensive was to take place over already devastated ground. Each rifleman carried 57.5Ibs and a Lewis gunner 73Ibs. The weather was getting worse, with the British having to move their artillery forward into the area devastated by shellfire and soaked by the autumn rains, restricting the routes on which guns and ammunition could be moved, presenting German artillery with easier targets. No formal artillery preparation was conducted before 4th October, except for the normal heavy artillery counter-battery fire and destructive fire on German strong-points.

The 7th Battalion was part of the 11th Division, XVIII Corps on the northern part of the line. Within the 11th Division the 33rd Brigade would advance on the left, but part of a five Brigade frontage in the XVIII Corps area, stretching north to south, from 86 Brigade (29th Division) 10th Brigade and 11th Brigade (4th Division) and then 33rd and 34th Brigade (11th Division). Within 33rd Brigade there was a two-battalion frontage, with the 9th Sherwood Foresters on the left and 7th South Staffordshire Regiment on the right. On the right on the 7th South Staffordshire Regiment were the 11th Manchesters as part of the 34th Brigade. Behind the front line were the 6th Border Regiment as the Brigade Reserve and the 6th Lincoln Regiment as the Divisional reserve. In direct support of the Brigade were the 33rd Machine Gun Company, and the 33rd Light Trench Mortar Battery. During the initial assault the guns of 32nd, 34th and 197th Machine Gun Companies were also firing in support of the Brigade, so over forty machine guns on a very small frontage. In addition, ten tanks of D Battalion, 1st Tank Brigade were in support of the assault to breach the enemy wire and trench lines.

The artillery plan had the first belt of creeping barrage beginning 150 yards beyond the jumping-off tapes. During the pause the barrage was to move 1,000 yards further to hit German counterattacks and then suddenly return. At zero plus 130 minutes, it was to advance in 100 yards lifts every eight minutes to the final objective. After another pause the barrage was to creep forward at hourly intervals for 1,500 yards into the German defences. The defensive barrage by the first two belts from the field artillery was to stop at 11:20 except for SOS fire and the two back belts of heavy and medium artillery at 13:44 Smoke was used at high ground about Meunier House, in addition a Gas shell bombardment at zero plus 4.45 to zero plus 6.45 was to be used to disrupt any enemy Counterattacks.

The 7th Battalion has a list of eleven strong points listed as objectives, of the concrete bunker type they had been training to assault in the rear area. These were given code names to allow companies to report once they were taken. The battalion was to be formed up in their battle positions and all arrangements complete for the advance by zero minus one hour. The necessity of maintaining silence while forming up will be firmly impressed on all ranks and once the troops are formed up, there was to be no further movement.

From the middle of 1917, the area east of Ypres was defended by six German defensive positions, the front line, *Albrechtstellung* (second position), *Wilhelmstellung* (third position), *Flandern I Stellung* (fourth position), *Flandern II Stellung* (fifth position) and *Flandern III Stellung* (under construction). In between the German defence positions lay the Belgian villages of Zonnebeke and Passchendaele. All available machine-guns including those of the support and reserve battalions of the front-line regiments, were sent into the forward zone to form a cordon of four to eight guns every 250 yards. Ground holding divisions were reinforced by the *Stoß* regiment of each of the *Eingreif* divisions. These were moved up behind each front division into the artillery protective line, which backed on to the forward battle zone, to launch earlier counterattacks while the British were consolidating. The bulk of the *Eingreif* divisions were to be held back and used for a methodical counterattack on the next day or the one after and for spoiling attacks between British offensives. Gas bombardment was to be increased on forward infantry positions and artillery emplacements whenever the winds allowed. Every effort was to be made to induce the British to reinforce their forward positions, where the German artillery could engage them. Operation High Storm (*Unternehmen Höhensturm*), a bigger German organised counterattack, intended to recapture the area around Zonnebeke which had been planned for 3 October, but was postponed for a day.

The 7th battalion had formed up on the start line by 4.52. 06:00 was zero hour, with the battalion shaken out with A Company on the left, with platoons forward, and B Company on the right with one platoon forward. With this three-platoon frontage, D and B company formed a second wave with C Company in reserve. Whilst waiting for the go, at 05:30 an enemy shell between Pheasant Farm and Snipe House caused considerable casualties of reserve. On H-hour the battalions attacked with mixed in with their support tanks and a creeping barrage. Four were killed and 12 wounded on the approach to the jump off line. For the attack, the British made heavy use of gas. 6am was zero hour, and casualties were suffered immediately, with 2nd Lieutenants White and Taylor killed on the start line. Roger Taylor was an officer of A Company, and was greatly liked by all ranks.

For the next few hours, the battalion moved forward along with the remainder of the division. The 7th Battalion had an easy advance to the intermediate line and then overcame small parties of German infantry concealed in shell-holes. Fire from the church and the Brewery pillbox in Poelcappelle caused a delay but Gloster Farm was captured with the aid of two tanks and the red line (first objective) consolidated. Troops from the inner flanks of both brigades and several tanks entered Poelcappelle and then captured pillboxes beyond the east end. A shelter was captured near the church in Poelcappelle amid sniper fire. Ferdan House was captured and the final objective consolidated. D Company, in the lead reported objectives secure at 7.16am. The second objectives was captured at 8.55am. Tanks had assisted the assault, and the battalion used them to carry the infantry in some cases, which proved successful. By 13:00 the objectives of the battalion had all been taken.

During the initial attack, the battalion lost three officers and 32 soldiers were killed, with 153 soldiers wounded. The company aid posts were heavily hit, with the company sergeant majors of A and B Company, Company Sergeant Major Smitheman and Company Sergeant Major Crump killed. The Battalion Padre Major the Reverand W C Wilkes MC was also killed in the aid post by a shell splinter, he had been with the 11th Division since 1914. Sergeant Thomas Craddock moved to the company aid post and coordinate the extraction of the casualties to the rear areas whilst the advance was ongoing. In the advancing companies, casualties amongst the officers and Senior NCOs were especially heavy, with one captain killed, along with three subalterns, four sergeants and three corporals. Testament to the experience of the soldiers in the battalion was that this did not hold up the advance, and many junior leaders stepped forward to lead. This was later reflected in the awarding of medals.

A counterattack at 13:00 was defeated and reinforcements allowed the new line to be established between the Steenbeek and the Langemarck–Winnipeg Road. A resumption of the attack at 17:00 was cancelled due to rain and poor light. The capture of the ridges was a great success and General Plumer called the attack "... the greatest victory since the Marne" and *Der Weltkrieg*, the German official history, referred to "... the black day of October 4". There had been an average advance of 1,000 yards across the front and most objectives were taken. The British artillery fired a standing barrage for two and a half hours while the infantry dug in undisturbed and German counterattacks were dispersed with artillery fire.

The battalion held the position and on 8th October 1917 was pulled from the line by the 9th West Yorkshire Regiment. On 22nd October 1917 the battalion relived the 11th Essex Regiment on the left-hand side of the Brigade frontage. The battalion was under strength, at 28 officers and 743 men. During the week in the line, the battalion sent patrols forward and conducted work on a sap in the line. On the 30th the battalion was relieved by the 8th Duke of Wellington's Regiment and moved to the rear areas at Verquin. Even in this quiet spell, the battalion suffered three killed and eight wounded through the routine combat on the front line.

The battalion moved to the rear areas to consolidate and receive fresh reinforcements. The battalion would remain in the rear until 21st November. On 1st November 1917 Sergeant 17778 Thomas Charles Craddock was informed at Verquin, that he was to be awarded the Military Medal for his actions on the battlefield on 4th November 1917. 24men in the battalion were awarded the Military Medal this day, stepping up when the first line of leadership were cut down in the advance.

Chapter 8
Trench Raid

November started with a period of training in the rear area, with the battalion then moving up to the reserve area of the Lens sector, relieving the 9th Sherwood Foresters on the night of 7th November. The battalion would serve on this Lens-Loos area for the next month. They were billeted in cellars in the rear areas. A Company and Sergeant Craddock were however in the reserve trench. On 8th November the remainder of the Brigade conducted a raid on the front. This was followed by a dummy attack on the 10th to draw the enemy into the open. The patrols and raids continued through the week, with a steady trickle of casualties amongst the companies.

On 18th November 1917 A and B Companies of the battalion received orders to move to St Pierre for a trench raid. A preliminary set of orders were received:

Secret
7th Battalion South Staffordshire Regiment

Operational Order No. 56

1. Preliminary operational order No. 56 is cancelled and the following substituted.

2. At zero on a date and time to be notified later A and B Companies will attack the enemy's 1st and 2nd line trench system on a frontage of 370 yards between the following points. 1st Line (CINNEBAR Trench) from junction of CINNEBAR TRENCH and NUN'S ALLEY to the junction of CINNEBAR and

NAG Trenches. 2nd Line (NUNS ALLEY and NAG TRENCH) The attack will be supported by artillery and a Machine Gun Barrage. The objectives of the attack are as follows:

(1) *To obtain identification*

(2) *To kill or capture as many of the enemy as possible*

(3) *To capture or destroy hostile Trench Mortars, Machine Guns, Dugouts, Stores etc*

3. *Dispositions.*

(a) B Company consisting of 3 officers and 1000 other ranks will capture the enemy 1st line between the boundaries stated above.

(b) A Company (supplemented by 15 ranks of B Company and 1 Sergeant and 35 ranks of C Company) with a total of three officers and 156 other ranks will capture the enemy 2nd line.

(c) Captain W H Tosdevinem will be in command of both companies attacking and will be OC Raid.

4. *Assembly and Forming Up. Both companies will be formed for the attack by zero minus 30 minutes. B Company will form up on our front line (CARP Trench) and along a line to be taped out in continuation of CARP Trench southwards and parallel to their objectives. The left of this company will rest at the junction of CANTEEN and CARP Trenches and its right a point 100 yards south of CARP Trench.*

5. *Direction. The direction of the advance will be 90 degrees true bearing for the left and right of both companies. The centre will direct. Two short tapes laid in the direction of the advance will be placed on each flank of the forming*

up line. In addition, two boards painted white will have been placed on either flank half way across no man's land to correct direction during the advance.

6. Division of Tasks.

    (a) OC B Company will detail three parties of 1 NCO and 8 men each. One of these parties will be placed on the left flank and one on the right and the third in the centre. The party of the left will be responsible for establishing and holding a block in CINNEBAR Trench north of the Trench Junctiopn. The centre party will establish and hold a block 50 yards up NABOB Trench. The right party will be responsible for establishing and holding a block in CINNEBAR Trench south of the trench junction and also in NAG and NEW Trenches. These parties will advance straight to the point allotted to them, but they will nevertheless be responsible for dealing with any opposition which is met during the advance. Of the remaining men of b Company, 40 will advance on the north side and 30 on the south side of NABOB Trech. The Company Commander will establish his HQ at the junction of CINNEBAR and NABOB Trenches.

    (b) OC A Company will detail a party of 1 NCO and 9 men who will be responsible for establishing and holding a block in NABOB trench not more than 20 yards east of the junction of NAG Trench and NUNs alley. Two Lewis gun teams of 6 other ranks will be detailed to take up positions on the enemy parados, one 50 yards north and one fifty yards south of the junction of NUNS ALLEY, NABOB and NAG Trenches. The position of these guns will be governed by the field of fire obtainable which, if possible, should be all round. Six good shots will also be detailed t take up positions on the enemy parados to assist

Lewis Gunners as necessary. Of the remaining men of A Company 60 will advance on the north and 60 on the south of Nabob.

Of those advancing north of NABOB 15 other ranks will follow along the north side of NUNS ALLEY after its junction will CINNEBAR Trench.

Of those advancing south of NABOB 15 other ranks will follow along the south side of NAG after its junction with CINNEBAR Trench.

OC A Company will establish his HQ in NABOB Trench 50 yards west of the junction of NUNS ALLEY, NABOB and NAG Trenches. Captain Tosdevine will establish his HQ in a T Trench off NABOB Trench.

B Company will advance in extended order the NCOs and men detailed for special details being slightly less extended than the remainder.

A Company will form up in line of small columns of file. After crossing the 1st objective these columns will form an extended line with the exception of those detailed to advance on the north side of NUN'S ALLEY and those on the south side of NAG.

The detailed orders gave little to be considered and were drawn from many years of combat experience by the battalion. However, they were very complex, and gave little room for the various commanders in the company to use initiative. With such specific tasks given to subunits within companies, if one element went wrong, then various routes out and in of the enemy trench would be left exposed.

The remainder of the order detailed specific elements to the operations, such as the removal of all markings, documents and papers before the assault and the issuing of a raid disk to identify the soldier. All ranks were to carry two bombs, and each company would have ten 'P' Bombs and ten Mobile charges. 'P' Bombs were a red phosphorous bomb. A Company would be armed with 20 trench bridges to cross the first line and exploit into the second line. Looting parties were delegated, as well as stretcher bearers and runners. 12 men in each company had torches attached to bayonets for searching dug outs.

The night before the raid, an update arrived:

Secret
7th Battalion South Staffordshire Regiment

Amendment to Operational Order No. 56

1. Zero will be at 0615am tomorrow November 21st 1917.

2. A and B Companies will leave St Pierre at 2am on the 21st and will proceed to the front line as follows. Parties from both companies will form up North of Nabob via C Company Route and CANTEEN ALLEY. Parties of both Companies to form up North of Nabob via C Company on Route COWLEY and CONDUCTOR.

Guides. OC C Company and D Company have detailed four guides to lead parties by the following routes.

69

- *C Company Guides C route COWLEY and CONDUCTOR*
- *D Company Guides C Route CANTEEN ALLEY*

3. A and B Companies will not fix bayonets till the barrage commences.

4. All stores for use by A and B Companies will be issued before leaving St Pierre. OC A and B Companies will arrange that hot soup is served before leaving and that breakfast is ready in St Pierre at 9am.

5. Raid discs will be issued under arrangement made by OC A and B Companies. All ranks will carry their raid discs in the right breast pockets of their tunics.

6. Stretcher Bearers. Lieutenant H Masson will report to the MO at Battalion Headquarters   at 2am. Stretcher bearers of C and D Companies together with reserve men and an additional four men per company will report to at Battalion Headquarters   at 2am. Stretcher bearers of A and B Companies will fall out at Battalion Headquarters   as their company passes and report to the MO.

7. Synchronization of Watches. 2nd Lieutenant Holloway will report to Brigade HQ at 10pm tonight on the 20th to synchronise watches. This officer will then visit Captain W H Tosdevine and OC A and B Companies in St Pierre after which he will report to Battalion Headquarters   where he will remain until further notice.

8. Patrols. As soon as A and B Companies arrive in the front-line OC C and D Companies will each send a patrol of one officer and three other ranks. These patrols will ensure that none of the enemy approaches our lines. They will return at zero minus 5 minutes.

9. <u>Prisoners</u>. 2nd Lieutenant Dixon will meet 12 men to be detailed by OC A Company 9th Sherwood Foresters at Battalion Headquarters at 5am and will then proceed to the junction of COWLEY and CHICORY Trenches as already stated.

10. <u>Police</u>. OC A Company 9th Sherwood Foresters will detail 20 men and will post then at the following points:

> *Junction of HAPPY and CARFAXT Trenches*
> *Junction of CARFAX and CANTEEN Trenches*
> *Junction of DOUGLAS and COWLEY Trenches*
> *Junction of COWLEY and COMMOTION Trenches*
> *Junction of CALLIPER and CONDUCTIOR Trenches*
> *Junction of CONTROL and CATAPULT Trenches*
> *Junction of CUTOFF and COMMOTION Trenches*

These men will be in position at 6am, during the withdrawal they will direct all men to the rendezvous in COUNTER trench and also collect raid discs. These will then be handed into Battalion Headquarters by OC A Company 9th Sherwood Foresters. On completion of the withdrawal OC B Company will detail one man who is not taking part in the raid. This man will be on duty at Reserve Battalion Headquarters and will collect all men who have missed their way to the rendezvous in COUNTER Trench. He will collect raid discs from these men.

W H Carter

Lieutenant Colonel

Commanding

7th Battalion South Staffordshire Regiment

The two companies arrived at St Pirre at about 06:00, breakfast was served immediately on arrival. Raid stores were issued during the day, including mobile charges which were fitted with fused by the Royal Engineers. Ladders were issued to A Company to moved to the area of the German Front line. Orders were issued that the raid would take place on the 21st with a zero hour of 06:15. Guides from C and D Company reported to the OC of the raid to guide the companies to the jumping-off line.

A and B Companies left St Pierre at 01:00, B Company leading and arrived at Battalion Headquarters at 04:00. Forming up was delayed for a while owing to the guides losing their way. This was rectified however, and the forming took place without incident. The code word for formed up reached Battalion Headquarters at 05:50, the raiding party took off at zero hour and at zero plus 6 mins, B Company under the command of Lieutenant Freeman arrived in the 1st Objective.

At this point, as per the orders, cut offs were placed at either end of the enemy trenches, and the detailed clearance started. The cut offs on each end of the trench were one NCO and eight men, these men held the end of the enemy trench and prevented enemy from counterattacking. Each enemy dug out was approached and the enemy were shouted at to surrender. If they refused a 'P Bomb' was used first, if the enemy then still refused, a mobile charge was dropped down the entrance, destroying it and most likely the entire dug out. For those dug outs where the enemy surrendered, the first five prisoners were sent back to Battalion Headquarters, but the remainder were moved to the front line and held there during the raid. Those empty dugouts were then searched by men who had torches on their bayonets and then by the looting party to gain enemy items of significance.

As the enemy 1st line trench was entered at zero plus 6 minutes, the bombardment of the second line had started, this continued until zero plus 12 when it creeped into depth. A Lewis gun barrage was fired 500 yards from the 2nd line trenches to suppress the enemy and prevent counterattacks. Unfortunately, A Company under the command of Captain F K Lindner lost direction and did not gain the objective. They crossed the first line trenches in columns using the trench bridges, but as the company split, they became lost in the open ground. At this point both Captain Linder commanding A Company and Lieutenant Freeman commanding B Company were wounded adding to the confusion of the situation.

The exception to this lost company was of half a platoon commanded by Sergeant Craddock and a Lewis gun section under Sergeant Griffin. Both these NCOs pushed on towards the 2nd line trenches. However, although they managed to enter the trench from the northern flank and place the Lewis guns on the parapet to supress in depth, they were forced to withdraw owing the lack of support by the remainder of the company. Without the cut offs to the south, and without enough troops to secure all of the trench, they could not complete their objectives. They made the difficult decision to pull back.

The Lewis guns under Sgt Griffin waited until Sgt Craddock's platoon was 50 yards in the open before they started to pull back. The men of B Company and those from A Company now in the first line trenches also pulled back. All troops were back in their own front line in less than 45 minutes. Casualties were 7 dead and 30 wounded. Amongst the killed were 2nd Lieutenant G

Vaughan and Sgt Edwards, and amongst the wounded were Captain J F Lindner and Lieutenant J Freeman. One NCO and six soldiers were missing in action during the raid. That following night the battalion was relieved by the 9th Sherwood Foresters, and they moved to billets in Noeux Les Mines. Sergeant Craddock was appointed acting Company Sergeant Major and would manage the company day to day from this point forward.

In 1917 the battalion had lost 218 soldiers, and many more were wounded. This included six new 2nd Lieutenants who had joined since Gallipoli, but also Captain Robert Charlton who had been awarded the Military Cross and Lieutenant Taylor who were more experienced. Company Sergeant Major McGrath had been killed along with six sergeants, including Sergeant Yates who had been awarded the Military Medal. 33 Junior NCOs had been killed, including Corporal Fisher who had been awarded the Distinguished Conduct Medal and Corporal Percy Hendley who had been awarded the Military Medal. Such losses again were hard to suffer for the battalion, and constant fresh faces appeared to replace those who had fought in the Mediterranean. Of the Private Soldiers killed, four were awarded Military Medals this year, including Private Harry Bellfield from Wolverhampton and Private Sutton from Tipton. And of course, Private Thomas Barrat who was later awarded the Victoria Cross.

Chapter 9
1918

January 1918 found the battalion in the rear areas conducting drill and training as part of 11th Division. The battalion was very low on manpower with an effective strength of only 20 officers and 558 other ranks. On Sunday 6th January 1918, Acting Company Sgt Major Craddock was presented with the Military Medal by the General Officer Commanding of the 11th Division. From 16th January, reinforcements started to arrive, with seven new 2nd Lieutenants joining the battalion to replace recent losses, but large numbers were not forthcoming in terms of other ranks.

On 28th January 1918 in the London Gazette the award of the Military Medal to Sgt Craddock was announced. On the same day, the battalion moved to the front line, relieving the 9th Sherwood Foresters in the Hullock sector, one mile north of Loos which they would now occupy for seven consecutive months.

On 30th January, the Mons Medal '1914 star' was announced. Of those in the battalion four officers, one Warrant Officer three SNCOs, ten JNCOs and eighteen private soldiers were eligible. On the 4th February one of the battalions in the 33rd Infantry Brigade, the 6th Battalion the Border Regiment, was broken up, providing reinforcements to other units, with the brigade having now only three battalions, the 7th South Staffordshire Regiment, 9th Sherwood Foresters and 6th Lincolnshire Regiment. Such measures showed the lack of manpower available to Britain at this time.

Although not on the front line, work parties were in support of the wider brigade, and under the enemy artillery Private Barton was killed and six other soldiers wounded. For the next week, enemy artillery caused low level casualties across the battalion and by the end of the month, the battalion had 27 officers and 607 men, but only 468 of these were 'trench strength', so those serving in the front line, rather than support roles. The greatest impact was the constant loss of officers and Senior NCOs, in February alone, with no major actions, two officers and one sergeant were amongst the wounded. On 23rd February, the 8th (Service) Battalion of the South Staffordshire Regiment was disbanded, with many of the soldiers joining the 7th Battalion.

On 1st March the battalion were again on the front line, with A Company occupying four posts along the trench line. Enemy trench mortars fired routinely, with some small enemy patrols of less than ten men. The battalion remained on the front line until 11th March and during this time, 3 men were killed and seven wounded, including a new 2nd Lieutenant. The routine of the quiet front line was only broken up by a small raiding party led by 2nd Lieutenant Stocking of D Company with 35 other ranks on the enemy front line on the night of 9th March. On 10th March the enemy used Mustard Gas on the front line, but no casualties were suffered.

On 13th March 1917 the battalion were pulled back to the reserve area at Mazingarae to conduct training but returned to the front line on the 16th. The first reinforcements for four months arrived with 49 other ranks from the 11th Division reinforcement camp, which included many experienced soldiers returning from their wounds. From the 18th shelling increased on the front line, with enemy trench mortars and gas shells being used. This continued up to the 19th, but the battalion still conducted active patrols and work fatigues. A Canadian battalion on the right flank was raided on the night of 19th March causing 30 casualties.

At 05:20 on Wednesday 20th March, a heavy barrage came down on the front right company, with a mixture of high explosive and mustard gas. 16 casualties were caused, including Sgt Garratt and a new 2nd Lieutenant. At 08:30 enemy aeroplanes dropped six, 20Ib bombs on the trenches, killing two soldiers and wounding Sergeant Bell and Private Owens.

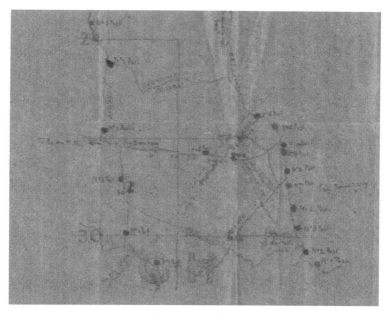

Image 9: Operations March 1918 (Battalion War Diary)

By 21st March, news was coming through of a large-scale German offensive by 30 division across a 50 mile front within 3rd Army. However, the line at Loos apart from the increased bombardments was relatively quiet. Orders were given to build up defensive and place small arms ammunition at forward points. By the 24th, the 46th Division had taken over the right flank of the battalion requiring new liaisons to occur. Over the next few days reinforcements arrived brining the battalion strength up to 763 men, of which 638 were front line trench strength. By Easter Sunday on 31st March 1917, there had been no offensive in the 7th Battalion's sector, and expectations of an enemy attack were reduced.

As April continued, the front line continued with low level shelling, gas attacks and trench mortars. On 10th April 1918, 1st Army sent out a general warning of an enemy offensive, but in the end no offensive took place in the Loos sector. On 24th April, a local relief of the enemy to the front was sighted and disrupted by the battalion. Throughout the month, the constant casualties due to artillery continued.

On 2nd May 1918 the battalion was relieved on the front line by the 8th Battalion of the Northumberland Fusiliers, 34th Brigadee and went into reserve. They were given huts at Mazingarbe, and as a battalion spend the 3rd May cleaning up. Training started on 4th May with physical training, musketry and the firing range. One soldier, Private Rife was wounded by a gas shell which fell on the training ground.

The 5th May was a Sunday. and the Commander of 11th Division, Major General H R Davies presented medals to the battalion, including a military cross and bar to 2nd Lieutenant H Piggims and six military medals, including to Sgt Arnold. Company Sergeant Major Craddock organised A Company for the parade having smartened them up as much as possible from the front.

On 6th May 1918, whilst A Company was training at Mazingerbe, a chance shell (British) fell amongst the soldiers. Acting Company Sergeant Major Craddock was killed. Private Pardoe later died of wounds. A further seven were wounded. An instantaneous fuse was the cause of so many casualties being inflicted by one shell.

Thomas was buried at Mazingarbe cemetery on the following day 7th May 1918 with full military honours.

We have received the following account of the burial in France behind the lines of a gallant warrant officer of the South Staffordshire Regiment. Relatives of men who have fallen will be comforted to read of the Christian burial accorded our men by their comrades when circumstances permit.

On May 7th in a little village behind the line, the funeral took place of Company Sergeant Major T Craddock MM, A Company, 7th Battalion South Staffordshire Regiment. He was killed the day previously by a chance shell whilst his battalion was back in reserve. It was impressive site to see the slow march to the graveyard, the chaplain in his full clerical robes proceeding the beir, which draped in the Union Jack was borne by six Senior NCOs of the battalion. Behind the beir came every single man of A Company with a firing party of twelve marching with arms reversed. Last in the procession was the battalion band playing the dead march in 'Saul'. At the graveside was a very large number of mourners, including the Commanding Officer, Lieutenant Colonel W H Carter DSO MC, the Second in Command, Adjutant, Company Commanders and the Regimental Sergeant Major. And practically every officer and senior NCO of the battalion.

Before the service started a beautiful wreath of narcissus lilac and cherry blossom was placed on the beir. The card was simply inscribed 'From the Officers of Headquarters Mess'. When the short but beautiful service had been read, the firing party fired three volleys over the grave and then stood at present whilst the bugles played 'The

Last Post' the large congregation standing rigidly to attention. Thus a fitting last tribute was paid to one of our bravest comrades, a man admired and respected throughout the battalion. May he rest in peace.

The battalion continued training for the next three days and rejoined the line on 10th May, taking over from the 6th Battalion The Yorkshire Regiment.

Thomas' name appears in the Walsall roll of honour and an account of his funeral was published in the Walsall Observer and Pioneer on 18th May 1918 and 26th June 1918. Thomas was entitled to the Military Medal, 1914-15 Star, the 1914-18 Victory medal and the 1914-18 War Medal. His final rank was Acting Warrant Officer 2nd Class. Company Sergeant Major, A Company, 7th Battalion, the South Staffordshire Regiment. He is buried in plot 3, Row C, Grave 7 in Mazingarbe communal cemetery extension, France. He was 31 years old when he died.

Chapter 10
Epilogue

The 7th Battalion remained in the Loos sector for the remainder of June and July. The battalion fought at the Battle of the Drocourt-Quant Line and the Battle of the Hindenburg Line. At the armistice, the battalion was on high ground east of Havay. Throughout the war, they has suffered huge losses, with 672 killed, and many more wounded. The last soldier to die in action was Private Charles Kendall Mardle who was the third son of Mr and Mrs G. Mardle, of Derby, England and husband of Kathleen Mardle, of 42, Eden Street, Alvaston, Derby. He died of shell fire on the 9th November 1918. However, before the disbandment, a further six soldiers would die directly of their wounds in November 1918.

The war took much from many of those who lived in the early twentieth century, and the Craddock's were one more family who suffered at this time. Thomas wrote a postcard to his mother before he was killed;

Dear Mother

Pleased to tell you I am going on fine and hope you are in the best of health. I know you still live at the same address. I sent you a letter and please can you confirm you received them. With best love and wishes,

From Tom

Thomas' brother James was posted to 1st Battalion Loyal North Lancashire Regiment. He was on leave between 27th October 1917 and 6th November 1917, which would have been a happy reunion for his family. After he rejoined his battalion on 26th November 1917, he was wounded on 3rd October 1918. James died of wounds at 58th Casualty clearing station in France on Saturday 6th October 1918 age 40.

Thomas' other brothers served in the war; Frank served in the First World War in 3rd Battalion of the South Staffordshire Regiment. However, he was fortunate to have not served overseas in the war. Robert joined the Royal Navy Volunteer Reserve Bristol Division in 1917. He served on a minesweeper, The Frascati, and survived the war.

To have seen her sons have to go to war and two of them never return must have been terrible for Mary. For Mary, the changes in education, work and an end to the famine of the past, were a thing which by 1933 must have been very evident to her. Conditions had hugely improved with the reforms to the welfare state, education and working conditions after the war, despite the difficult economic times of the Great Depression. However, such an industrial war, which saw bombs drop on what was her hometown for most of her life, must have made her wonder and fear for the modern world too. Mary lived until 1933, and for the death of her two sons she received a payment from the Army totalling 19 shillings and 7 pennies. This would have been around £57 in today's money, or two days salary for Thomas in skilled tradesmen profession.

Thomas' father James passed away in 1924 at age 77. He had a long life for a man who had in the end 11 children and worked hard as both a tanner and labourer all of his life.

Image 10: CSM Thomas Craddock (Authors Collection)

The story of the 7th Battalion the South Staffordshire Regiment, and the story of Thomas Charles Craddock are but one unit and one man in a war of incredible scale. To go through such a terrible conflict, only to die its last months is a sad story which pulls at the heart strings. But in writing this book, I hope that you too will remember the suffering that occurred and why, no matter what, we should never let such a conflict occur again.

Annex A – Battalion Locations

Country	Location	Date From	Date To	Remarks
Britain	Wittington	15 Aug 1914	28 Aug 1914	
Britain	Grantham	28 Aug 1914	April 1915	
Britain	Frensham	April 1915	30 Jun 1915	
Movement by Ship				Empress of Britain
Greece	Mudros	21 Jul 1915	21 Jul 1915	
Movement by Ship				Italian Coaster Abushai
Ottoman Empire	Helles	22 Jul 1915	28 Jul 1915	
Movement by Ship				Osmanieh
Greece	Imbros	28 Jul 1915	6 Aug 1915	
Movement by Ship				Small landing craft
Ottoman Empire	Sulva Bay	6 Aug 1915	20 Dec 1915	
Movement by Ship				Derfflinger (Captured German Ship)
Greece	Imbros	20 Dec 1915	28 Jan 1916	
Movement by Ship				HMT Oriana
Egypt	Sidi Bishr (Alexandria)	2 Feb 1916	10 Mar 1916	
Egypt	Ballah (Suez Canal)	10 Mar 1916	1 July 1915	Garrison
Movement by Ship				HMT Minnewaska
France	Marseilles			
France	Arras Sector	15 Jul 1916	28 Aug 1916	
France	Somme Sector	1 Sep 1916		
France	Ancre Sector	9 Dec 1916		
France	Cramont	18 Jan 1917	18 Mar 1917	Railway Construction
France	Demicourt	18 Apr 1917	14 May 1917	
France	Messines	14 May 1917	14 Jun 1917	

	Sector			
France	Ypres	13 Jul 1917	22 Oct 1917	
France	Lens	22 Oct 1917	27 Dec 1917	
France	Hulluch	27 Dec 1917	25 Aug 1918	
France	Arras	25 Aug 1918	Sep 1918	
France	Cambrai	Sep 1918	Nov 1918	
France	Sambre	Nov 1918	Armistice	

Annex B – Formation Commanders

Commanders 11th Northern Infantry Division

Rank	Name	First Name	Date From	Date To	Reason
Lieutenant General	Fanshawe	Sir Edward	Aug 1914	Jul 1916	Promotion
Lieutenant General	Woolcombe	Sir Charles	Jul 1916	Dec 1916	
Brigadier General	Erskine	J	Dec 1916	Dec 1916	Acting
Major General	Richie	Archibald	Dec 1916	22 Apr 1917	Wounded in Action
Major General	Davies	Henry	22 Apr 1917	Sep 1918	Wounded in Action
Brigadier General	Winter	Sir Ormonde	Sep 1918	Sep 1918	Acting
Major General	Davies	Henry	Sep 1918	1919	

Commanders 33rd Infantry Brigade

Rank	Name	First Name	Date From	Date To	Reason
Brigadier General	Hodson		Sep 1914	15 Dec 1915	Killed in Action
Brigadier General	Hill	J	15 Dec 1915	26 Dec 1915	Temp Command
Brigadier General	Erskine		26 Dec 1915	Feb 1916	Posting
Brigadier General	Davies	H R	Feb 1916	22 Apr 1917	Field Promotion
Brigaider General	Daily	A C			

					Officer
Captain	Cowap	W T	17 Aug 1916	18 Sep 1916	Sick to England
Captain	Tosdevine	W H	20 Dec 1916	8 Nov 1918	Taken off Strength
Captain	Morris		8 Nov 1917	1 Jan 1918	
Captain	Tosdevine	W H	1 Jan 1918	30 Jul 1918	
Captain	Freeman	J F F	30 Jul 1918	Feb 1919	Demobilised

Annex D – Known Warrant Officers of The Battalion - Appointments

Regimental Sergeant Major

Rank	Name	First Name	Date From	Date To	Home Town	Remark
RSM	Cowap		4 Aug 1914	?		
RSM	Mee	Francis Henry	?	22 Aug 1915		Killed i Actior
RSM	Griffiths	T	22 Aug 1915	March 1917		Woundec Action a Posted to (for commiss
RSM	Purchase		27 May 1917	Feb 1919	Brownhills	Woundec 1917 but in pos

Regimental Quartermaster Sergeant

Rank	Name	First Name	Date From	Date To	Home Town	Rem
WO2	Walker	E	4 Aug 1914	26 Jan 1916		Pron to (
			26 Jan 1916	Feb 1919		

Captains

Name	First Name	Coy	Joined Battalion	Left Battalion	Remarks
Bailey	C V	A and C	1914	12 Mar 1917	Sick and return to England
Baillon	J A MC	A and BHQ	Feb 1915	Feb 1919	Demobilisation
Burnett	E P S		Nov 1916	Nov 1917	To Tank Corps
Charlton	R	A	10 Nov 1915	4 Oct 1917	Killed in Action
Charrington	C E W	C	24 Dec 1918	Feb 1919	Demobilised
Christian	Edward Charles	D / BHQ	Nov 1914	11 Sep 1916	Killed in Action
Cowap	W T	D	20 May 1916	14 Dec 16	Wounded in Action
Crick	L C	C	23 Sep 1915	23 Nov 16	Posted Lincolns
Florey	B W P	A	Dec 1914		
Forrest	H	C	25 Apr 1917	Jan 1919	Demobilised
Freeman	F L	C	12 Jan 1916	21 Jul 1918	Transferred VIII Corps Staff
Freeman	J F F	B	10 Nov 1915	1919	Demobilised
Grice-Hutchinson	C	B	5 Oct 1915	27 Sep 1916	Wounded in Action
Hume	Edward Archibald		Unknown	27 Aug 1915	Killed in Action
Hutchinson	C		2 Dec 1915	9 Apr 1916	Transferred 6 Lincolns Adjt
Harland	C C		26 Dec 1916	17 Mar 1918	Transferred 85th Bde
Jones	R V	C	6 Aug 1917	13 Nov 1917	Transferred Bde TO
Legge	The Hon. Gerald		Unknown	09 Aug 1915	Killed in Action
Legge (the Hon)	G	D	Sep 1914	9 Aug 1915	Killed in Action
Linder	F J D	D / A	Nov 1914	3 Jul 1916	Return to base duty
Martin	H C	A	Sep 1914	9 Aug 1915	Killed in Action
Massey	C I	C	Jul 1918	1919	Demobilised

Morris	C M	BHQ	Sep 1914	9 Aug 1915	Killed in Action
Morris	F B	B	Apr 1917	Feb 1918	Transferred XXII Corps
Raynsford	E	A	Apr 1915	Aug 1915	Sick to England
Ritchie	C O	BHQ	Sep 1914	Sep 1914	Returned to Depot
Smith	C N	BHQ	1 Sep 1916	Feb 1919	Demobilised
Smyly	A F	B	10 Jul 1918	Sep 1918	Appointed Courts Martial Officer
Tosdevine	W H	D	10 Jun 1916	30 Jul 1918	Taken Off Strength
Townsend	L G O	A	Nov 1914	09 Aug 1915	Killed in Action
Worcester	Harold Paul	A	21 Sep 1915	10 Sep 1916	Killed in Action
Williams	G C	A	14 Sep 1915	17 Oct 1915	To England
Williams	W B	A	5 Oct 1915	Feb 1919	To staff of demobilisation camp

Lieutenants

Name	Name	Coy	Joined Battalion	Left Battalion	Remarks
Action	H	B Company	4th May 1918	Feb 1919	Killed in Action
Cox	E S		22 Nov 1916	Feb 1918	
Cundall	H A	D Company	Dec 1917	Jan 1918	Posted 1 S-Staffs
Dixon	A	B Company	6 Aug 1917	June 1918	Transferred 33rd TMB
Dixon	A M	A Company	1 Aug 1918	Jan 1919	Demobilized
Flinn	E C	D Company	7 Feb 1915	29 Oct 1915	Sick to England
Goldfinch	T M	A Company	5 Dec 1917	Feb 1919	Demobilised
Higgs	R D		19 Apr 1917	Feb 1919	Demobilised
Hutchinson	C D	B Company	5 Oct 1915	11 Mar 1916	Transferred to RFC
Isle	W C	D Company	Nov 1914	13 Aug 1915	Killed in Action
Jervis	F W S	D Company	8 Dec 1915	29 May 1916	
Kite	R	C Company	25 Nov 1918	1919	Demobilised
Laver	F R		7 Oct 1916	23 Oct 1916	Loaned to 32 Bde
Lawrence	G F	B Company	Nov 1914	Aug 1915	Sick to England
McGevor	J	QM Department	Aug 1914	3 Nov 1915	Sick to England
Marson	A E		6 Oct 1915	Jan 1919	Demobilised
Martin	J T	A Company	5 Dec 1917	March 1918	Wounded in Action
Masson	H R S	D Company	5 Oct 1915	Nov 1917	Sick to England
Moore	J A	B Company	Nov 1914	07 August 1915	Killed in Action
Parke	A	A Company	16 Mar 1916	7 Apr 1916	Returned to 9 Lanc Fus
Parkhouse	R	C	23 Nov	Dec 1918	Attached

		Company	1918		Construction Company
Pritchard	E W L		19 Feb 1917	1919	Demobilised
Proctor	C W	BHQ	8 Dec 1914	May 1918	Transferred to MG Corps
Raymond	A O		Sep 1918	24 Feb 1919	Return to Field Ambulance Unit
Rich	E R	B Company	31 Dec 1916	Feb 1919	Demobilised
Savory	W G T	HQ Coy	1 Sep 1916	5 Sep 1916	Loaned to 32 Bde
Shaw-Hellier	A B		Nov 1914	09 Aug 1915	Killed in Action
Simpson	C V	BHQ	1 Sep 1916	30 Jul 1918	Return to England
Summerton	Harold		Unknown	29 July 1915	Killed in Action
Spinney	R E		Jan 1917	Jan 1917	Killed in Action
Stanley	A H	D Company	10 Nov 1915	27 Nov 1915	Sick to England
Summerton	H	Scout Officer	Dec 1914	Jul 1915	Killed in Action
Taylor	Roger Cecil		21 Dec 1916	04 Oct 1917	Killed in Action
Thomas	P B	C Company	Sep 1915	Dec 1915	Sick to England
Thompson	Henry Thomas		Nov 1914	26 Sep 1915	Killed in Action
Walker	E	QM Department	26 Jan 1916	1919	Demobilised
Watson	M M	B Company	14 Jul 1917	Feb 1919	Demobilised
White	Edwin Victor	C Company	14 Apr 1916	06 Sep 1918	Missing in Action
Willoughby	J R		19 Dec 1916	1919	Demobilised
Wright	A E	BHQ	19 Dec 1916	Feb 1919	Demobilised

105

2nd Lieutenant

Name	Name	Coy	Joined Battalion	Left Battalion	Remarks
Anderson	E O	D	4 Feb 1918	Regular South Staffs	
Anderson	N L		Jun 1915	26 Sep 1916	Wounded in Action
Atkins	H G		7 Oct 1916	23 Oct 1916	Transferred to 32nd Bde
Barber		C	Feb 1919	Feb 1919	
Baylis	F S	A	12 Jun 1917	Feb 1919	Demobilised
Beattie	S M	A	1 Sep 1916	Sep 1916	Sick to England
Bennett-Evans	G L		1914	Feb 1917	Sick to England
Bonner	E A		Feb 1915	Jan 1917	To RAF
Bonner	G		Jan 1915	Jun 1915	To AA Section RFA
Bourne	A S	A	Nov 1915	26 Sep 1915	Wounded
Buchanan	F S	C	Oct 1915	21 Oct 1915	Hospital Sick
Burrell	H E	C	Oct 1915	27 Aug 1916	Sick to England
Bussy	J	C	Aug 1916	20 Sep 1916	Killed in Action
Carruthers	W A	D	16 Mar 1916	24 Jun 1916	11 Royal Scots
Carter	H W	A	11 July 1917	Sep 1917	Sick to England
Catterall	E C	B	16 Oct 1915	16 Dec 1915	Sick to England
Chapman	Sidney George	C	5 Oct 1915	28 Sep 1916	Killed in Action
Chatwin	H	B	11 Sep 1918	Jan 1919	Wounded (Gas)
Cleobury	S		19 Dec 1916	18 May 1917	To RFC
Cliff	R A	D	8 Aug 1916	29 Sep 1916	Wounded in Action
Coke	W R	B	16 Jan 1918	Feb 1918	To TM Btry
Cotterill	J	B	20 Oct 1916	Jun 1918	Substitution

Coxe	Eric Noel	B	9 May 1917	09 Jun 1917	Killed in Action
Davis	A D S	Scout Officer	6 Oct 1915	3 Mar 1916	Transfer RFC
Donnellan	T	D	6 Oct 1915	Jan 1917	Transfer E-Yorks
Donnelley	J L	A	8 Dec 1915	23 Dec 1915	Sick to England
Downing	J F	MG Officer	5 Oct 1915	4 Dec 1916	Transfer to RFC
Dryden	W B	A / B	14 Apr 1916	20 Aug 1917	Transferred to Salvage Coy
Duddell	A L		31 Jul 1916	1 Mar 1917	Transferred to RFC
Dumbleton	J E		11 Oct 1916	1 Mar 1917	Transferred to RFC
Dunn	G E	C	16 Mar 1916	19 Jun 1916	Transferred to Base Command
Eccles	E J	B	16 Mar 1916	20 Jun 1916	To Details
Edge	F S	D	11 Sep 1918	Jan 1919	Demobilised
Evans	N		4 Apr 1918	Jun 1918	Transferred to RAF
Evans	W F	D	19 Jul 1917	Aug 1917	Wounded in Action
Ford	H W	B	2 Nov 1917	14 Aug 1918	Transferred as Bde IO
Grant	B C	C	4 Feb 1918	May 1918	Wounded in Action (Gas)
Gwynne-Vaughan	K D	A	12 Jan 1916	6 Sep 1916	Killed in Action
Hall	E G	C	4 Sep 1918	Nov 1918	Wounded in Action
Hamner	H I		17 Oct 1915	2 Jun 1916	Transferred RFC
Harding	G A	C	4 Feb 1918	Feb 1919	Demobilised
Harrison	F F	B	4 Sep 1918	Oct 1918	Wounded in Action
Hartshorne	N H		6th Oct 1915	6 Aug 1916	Transferred 63 Div Gas Instr
Hollingsworth	F		1 Sep	23 Sep 1916	Loaned 32nd

			1916		Bde
Holloway	C E		6 Aug 1917	Oct 1918	Sick to England
Hoyle	H		8 Aug 1916	Mar 1918	Sick to England
Humphrey	E G	C	31 Jul 1916	Jan 1917	Loaned to RFC
Hunter	M A C		14 Sep 1915	14 Nov 1915	Killed in Action
Instone	Edwin Lloyd	D	11 Nov 1917	21 Jul 1917	PoW and then Died of Wounds
Jepson	B	A	16 Jan 1918	1919	Demobilised
Joels	W A	B	8 May 1916	20 Jun 1916	To Details
Johnson	H V	C	19 Dec 1916	19 Feb 1917	To E Yorks
Kay	H	C	8 Dec 1915	1 Apr 16	Transferred 33 MG Coy
Laughton	P S		4 Dec 1916	Feb 1917	Transfer to RFC
Lawrence	G F	C	Nov 1915	Aug 1915	Wounded in Action
Lewis	W E	B	13 Jun 1917	Sep 1917	Wounded in Action
Lloyd	B		Oct 1915	Oct 1915	Sick to England
Marshall	C	C	31 Dec 1916	27 July 1917	Killed in Action
Miller			Aug 1915	Aug 1915	Wounded in Action
Montgomery	C W	D	7 Oct 1916	Oct 1917	Return to England
Muirhead	L R		16 Mar 1916	20 Jun 1916	To details
Murphy			Aug 1915	Aug 1915	Wounded in Action
Nicholls	S C	D	23 Nov 1918	1919	Demobilised
Page	C L	B	18 Jul 1917	Jul 1917	Wounded in Action (Gas)
Palmer	L W	B	23 Nov 1918	Jan 1919	Demobilised
Piggins	H	C	16 Jan 1918	Jan 1919	Demobilised

Pugh	A E		23 Nov 1918	Jan 1919	Demobilised
Randle	W W	C	16 Jan 1918	Mar 1918	Wounded in Action
Richardson	H B	C	3 Feb 1916	20 Aug 1916	Transferred to MG Corps
Roberts	H E	B	16 Mar 1916	21 Jun 1916	To Details
Robson	G W	B	23 Nov 1918	Dec 1918	To 1st Army Agricultural School
Ronaldson	H H	C	Jan 1915	Aug 1916	Wounded in Action
Rowntree	C W	C	17 Feb 1916	Jul 1916	Wounded in Action
Rudge	W H	C	19 Apr 1918	1919	Demobilised
Sanders	H A		17 Sep 1916	25 Oct 1916	Loaned to 32 Bde
Scott	A E	A	Dec 1915	Jan 1918	Return to England
Settle	T L		12 Jan 1917	18 May 1917	Transfer to RFC
Shaw	E L	D	31 Dec 1916	1919	Demobilised
Shaw	J A		16 Mar 1916	4 May 1916	Returned to 9 Lancs Fusiliers
Sheppey	E T	B	11 Sep 1918	Dec 1918	Brigade Salvage Officer
Shone	P N		1 Sep 1916	18 May 1917	Transfer to RFC
Skesey	D		2 Oct 1917	24 Nov 1917	Sick to England
Small	E	BHQ	Jan 1915	Aug 1915	Wounded in Action
Smith	R G	A	10 Jul 1918	1919	Demobilised
Spencer-Cummings	J	C	17 Dec 1917	5 Jan 1918	Returned to England
Spicer	A C N		Dec 1914	Aug 1915	Wounded in Action
Squires	R A		Dec 1914	Aug 1915	Wounded in Action
Stanway	Gerald R		20 Oct	05 October	Killed in

			1916	1917	Action
Steele	W B	BHQ	11 Oct 1916	20 Dec 1916	Transferred RFC
Stocking	W	D	16 Jan 1918	1919	Demobilised
Sturt	E A		17 Feb 1916	4 Mar 1916	Transferred 33rd MG Coy
Summersscale	H		17 Feb 1916	6 Jun 1917	Wounded in Action
Taunton	Cuthbert Andre Patmore	B	3 Feb 1915	09 Aug 1915	Killed in Action
Thompson	H V	C	19 Dec 1916	Jul 1918	Wounded in Action
Tinkler	George Henry	A	19 Feb 1917	25 Apr 1917	Killed in Action
Vaughan	George William	B	30 Jul 1917	21 Nov 1917	Killed in Action
Vautier			7 Oct 1916	23 Oct 1916	Transferred 32 Bde
Watson	H		16 Mar 1916	21 Jun 1916	To details
Watts	C E	B	10 Feb 1918	Mar 1918	Wounded in Action
Wear	W	D	4 Feb 1918	Feb 1919	Demobilised
Webb	J D		1 Aug 1918	Jan 1919	Sick to England
Wedge	C N	B	19 Sep 1915	26 Oct 1915	Sick to Hospital
Weir	H K C		Oct 1915	Oct 1915	Died of Wounds
Welch	W H	B	10 Feb 1918	Nov 1918	Demobilised
West	G C	C	1 Sep 1916	Feb 1917	Accidently Killed
Wharram	C E	A	1 Apr 1917	Aug 1917	Transferred RFC
Wheeler	H G	B	23 Jan 1918	1919	Demobilised
White	C A	D	7 Sep 1916	4 Aug 1917	Killed in Action
White	J H		1 Sep 1916	Unknown	Loaned 32 Inf Bde
Whittle	D	B	12 Jan 1916	5 Oct 1917	Wounded in Action

Wickham	J C	A	23 Sep 1915	Nov 1915	Sick to Hospital
Winter	R H	A	8 Dec 1915	17 Dec 1915	Killed in Action
Yates	H	A	16 Jan 1918	Feb 1919	Demobilised
Youd	H	D	16 Jan 1918	Feb 1919	Demobilised

Annex F - Casualties of the 7th Battalion

Gallipoli 1915

Rank	Surname	Initials	Date Of Death
Corporal	Adams	C A	29/12/1915
Lance Serjeant	Anderson	C F E	11/12/1915
Lance Corporal	Andrews	W	09/08/1915
Private	Archer	J	09/08/1915
Private	Ashman	S	09/08/1915
Private	Astbury	W	09/08/1915
Private	Aston	A	07/08/1915
Private	Atterbury	A	09/11/1915
Private	Bailey	T L	11/08/1915
Private	Baker	T	08/08/1915
Private	Baker	W J	09/08/1915
Private	Banks	H	09/08/1915
Private	Barge	A	11/08/1915
Serjeant	Barnes	H	09/08/1915
Private	Barnett	J E	01/12/1915
Serjeant	Barratt	A	09/08/1915
Private	Barton	E	09/08/1915
Private	Bates	G	22/08/1915
Serjeant	Bayley	G	09/08/1915
Corporal	Bayliss	G	01/12/1915
Private	Beckwith	A E	09/08/1915
Lance Corporal	Belfield	A E	09/08/1915
Private	Bennett	H N	03/10/1915
Private	Beresford	A	13/01/1916
Private	Bird	E	09/08/1915
Private	Blincoe	A E	09/08/1915
Private	Bloomer	E	09/08/1915
Private	Blundell	J E	09/08/1915
Private	Blunt	R	09/08/1915
Lance Corporal	Box	W	22/08/1915
Private	Braden	A	09/08/1915

Private	Bradley	F	09/08/1915
Serjeant	Bradshaw	A	09/08/1915
Private	Brookes	D	09/08/1915
Private	Brown	J A	22/08/1915
Private	Brown	S	19/10/1915
Private	Bryan	A M	15/08/1915
Private	Burns	T	09/08/1915
Private	Burrason	D	23/08/1915
Private	Butler	J	08/08/1915
Corporal	Careless	A	17/10/1915
Private	Carney	P	09/08/1915
Lance Corporal	Carpenter	F	09/08/1915
Private	Carter	J	09/08/1915
Private	Cartwright	J	20/09/1915
Private	Cartwright	J J	25/11/1915
Private	Cash	A	23/08/1915
Private	Clark	J H	09/08/1915
Lance Corporal	Clark	A	31/12/1915
Private	Clayton	W	08/08/1915
Private	Clifton	V	09/08/1915
Private	Collier	C	09/08/1915
Private	Conway	P	25/07/1915
Private	Cooke	E T	21/09/1915
Private	Cooper	H	09/08/1915
Private	Cooper	J	09/08/1915
Private	Cooper	M S	22/08/1915
Private	Cope	J	09/08/1915
Lance Corporal	Corbett	A H	09/08/1915
Private	Cordwell	A V	01/09/1915
Private	Coster	J M	09/08/1915
Lance Corporal	Cresswell	G H	26/07/1915
Private	Cresswell	A J	22/08/1915
Lance Corporal	Critchley	J H	10/12/1915
Serjeant	Crudgington	C R	09/08/1915
Private	Darby	E	09/08/1915

Lieutenant Colonel	Daukes	A H	07/08/1915
Serjeant	Davis	G	23/08/1915
Private	Day	J	22/08/1915
Private	Dean	F	22/08/1915
Private	Double	J H	09/08/1915
Lance Corporal	Dunn	H	09/08/1915
Private	Dyke	H	22/08/1915
Private	East	W T	21/11/1915
Corporal	Edge	D	08/08/1915
Private	Edge	G R	22/08/1915
Private	Edwards	J	09/08/1915
Corporal	Edwards	E O	15/12/1915
Private	Elwell	J	09/08/1915
Corporal	Ennis	S	18/10/1915
Corporal	Evans	W	09/08/1915
Private	Evans	H L	22/08/1915
Private	Evans	H J	28/11/1915
Private	Evans	W H	10/12/1915
Private	Fellows	W	09/08/1915
Private	Fellows	B	09/08/1915
Private	Finch	J	09/08/1915
Lance Corporal	Fisher	A E	23/10/1915
Lance Corporal	Fleckner	F G	22/08/1915
Private	Fleet	G R	17/12/1915
Lance Corporal	Flint	W	03/11/1915
Lance Corporal	Ford	B	18/08/1915
Corporal	Forehead	T W	24/08/1915
Private	Freeman	J	09/08/1915
Serjeant	Gibbons	J	09/08/1915
Private	Gilbert	W	09/08/1915
Private	Gorton	H J	09/08/1915
Serjeant	Griffiths	A	09/08/1915
Lance Corporal	Griffiths	C	09/08/1915
Private	Grosvenor	W H	22/08/1915
Private	Hadley	C	11/12/1915

Private	Haley	G T	09/08/1915
Private	Hallwood	J	09/08/1915
Serjeant	Harris	F	09/08/1915
Private	Harris	E	27/08/1915
Private	Harris	J	08/09/1915
Private	Hawker	F	09/08/1915
Private	Haynes	S	09/08/1915
Private	Heath	I	09/08/1915
Serjeant	Hill	F	09/08/1915
Lance Corporal	Hodgkinson	H	08/08/1915
Private	Hodgkiss	S B	09/08/1915
Lance Corporal	Horseman	E G	05/12/1915
Private	Horsley	C	22/08/1915
Private	Hughes	S L	03/10/1915
Captain	Hume	E A	27/08/1915
Private	Hunter	T	09/08/1915
Lieutenant	Isle	W	13/08/1915
Private	Jackson	A	09/08/1915
Private	James	J	09/08/1915
Corporal	Jarvis	H T	24/08/1915
Private	Jasper	A	09/08/1915
Private	Jones	E F	09/08/1915
Private	Jones	W J	09/08/1915
Private	Jordan	J	09/08/1915
Private	Kelly	H	08/08/1915
Private	Kettle	J	22/08/1915
Private	Lee	T	22/08/1915
Private	Lee	J	05/09/1915
Captain	Legge	G	09/08/1915
Lance Corporal	Lewen	S W	09/08/1915
Private	Lewis	H	09/08/1915
Corporal	Lewis	W	20/10/1915
Private	Lloyd	A	02/08/1915
Private	Longmore	H	10/12/1915
Lance Corporal	Loynds	E E	09/08/1915

Private	Lucas	A	14/08/1915
Serjeant	Macham	A	09/08/1915
Private	Marshall	H	09/08/1915
Captain	Marten	H C	07/08/1915
Private	Martin	G H	08/08/1915
Private	Matthews	E	09/08/1915
Lance Corporal	Mcgauley	P	09/08/1915
Regimental Serjeant Major	Mee	F H	22/08/1915
Corporal	Merricks	G F	08/08/1915
Corporal	Mills	W G	22/08/1915
Private	Monington	A	22/08/1915
Lance Corporal	Montgomery	E	09/08/1915
Lieutenant	Moore	J A	07/08/1915
Captain	Morris	C M	09/08/1915
Private	Mosley	R J M	15/10/1915
Private	Murphy	J	09/08/1915
Private	Nelson	W	22/08/1915
Lance Corporal	Oakley	J	09/08/1915
Serjeant	O'connell	W	09/08/1915
Private	Oldham	W	09/08/1915
Private	Organ	A V	09/08/1915
Private	Owen	A	12/10/1915
Private	Palmer	G	09/08/1915
Private	Parkes	A	09/08/1915
Private	Patrick	H	09/08/1915
Private	Payne	S E	24/08/1915
Corporal	Peake	M	23/09/1915
Private	Pearce	J R	09/08/1915
Private	Peel	T	09/08/1915
Private	Pendrey	H M	09/08/1915
Private	Perkes	G	09/08/1915
Private	Perkins	H G	10/12/1915
Private	Perks	J	09/08/1915
Private	Perry	T J	09/08/1915
Private	Phillpot	H J	09/08/1915

Private	Pimm	W	09/08/1915
Private	Pitt	A	08/08/1915
Private	Pitt	J	24/08/1915
Private	Poole	E	09/08/1915
Private	Potts	N S	10/11/1915
Private	Powell	J	10/08/1915
Private	Powers	A	01/12/1915
Private	Poynton	R C	22/08/1915
Private	Pritchard	W	06/11/1915
Private	Ratcliffe	J	22/08/1915
Private	Ray	W	09/08/1915
Corporal	Reeves	R O	09/08/1915
Private	Roberts	I	22/08/1915
Private	Roberts	C	22/08/1915
Private	Rochell	W	24/11/1915
Private	Rollason	G	09/09/1915
Private	Rose	J	09/08/1915
Private	Sadler	G F	09/08/1915
Private	Shaw	B	09/08/1915
Corporal	Shaw	H W H	26/11/1915
Lieutenant	Shaw-hellier	A J B	09/08/1915
Lance Corporal	Shinton	G	09/08/1915
Lance Corporal	Sidebottom	H	11/12/1915
Lance Corporal	Slaney	C	01/09/1915
Lance Corporal	Small	A E	08/08/1915
Private	Small	G	16/10/1915
Lance Corporal	Smith	J	08/08/1915
Private	Smith	A	22/08/1915
Private	Spittle	A	22/08/1915
Private	Stockton	R	09/08/1915
Private	Stretton	C H	14/11/1915
Private	Stringer	H J	09/08/1915
Lieutenant	Summerton	H	29/07/1915
Private	Sutton	B	22/08/1915
Second Lieutenant	Taunton	C A P	09/08/1915

Private	Taylor	W H	09/08/1915
Private	Thompson	W	07/08/1915
Lieutenant	Thomson	H T	26/09/1915
Private	Thorpe	F A	01/09/1915
Private	Timmins	S	09/08/1915
Serjeant	Tomlinson	C E	09/08/1915
Corporal	Tonks	A	09/08/1915
Private	Townend	J W	09/08/1915
Captain	Townsend	L G O	09/08/1915
Private	Tranter	D	09/08/1915
Company Serjeant Major	Tresise	R G	09/08/1915
Private	Turley	J	13/10/1915
Private	Turner	G	09/08/1915
Private	Turner	T	09/08/1915
Private	Turner	H N	22/08/1915
Private	Tye	F	22/08/1915
Private	Walker	S	22/08/1915
Lance Corporal	Walker	J	12/10/1915
Lance Corporal	Waller	T	09/08/1915
Private	Walters	M	09/08/1915
Private	Walton	A	09/08/1915
Private	Ward	J H	09/08/1915
Serjeant	Warman	W J	22/08/1915
Private	Watson	O	22/08/1915
Lance Corporal	Webster	G	09/08/1915
Lance Corporal	Whitehead	S G	11/12/1915
Private	Whitehouse	T J	09/08/1915
Private	Wilson	A	09/08/1915
Private	Winfield	W	22/08/1915
Second Lieutenant	Winter	R H	17/12/1915
Lance Corporal	Wise	H	09/08/1915
Private	Wood	C	09/08/1915
Lance Corporal	Woodward	A	07/08/1915

France 1916 to 1918

Rank	Surname	Initials	Date Of Death
Private	Adams	J	23/08/1917
Private	Ainge	F	06/10/1918
Private	Aitken	J	04/10/1917
Private	Allen	E	25/11/1916
Private	Allen	D	27/11/1916
Lance Corporal	Allen	H	30/09/1916
Private	Allen	E J	27/07/1917
Corporal	Allen	J	19/08/1917
Serjeant	Ames	V	26/11/1916
Private	Amison	F	01/05/1917
Private	Anderson	J	31/07/1917
Private	Andrews	D	19/08/1917
Private	Andrews	J W	04/10/1917
Private	Anslow	G F	16/12/1916
Private	Ashby	W	10/02/1918
Private	Ashton	T H	26/07/1917
Lance Corporal	Athersmith	C	16/12/1916
Private	Baker	G E	28/09/1916
Private	Baker	A	07/06/1917
Private	Baker	J W	04/10/1917
Private	Baldock	W T	10/06/1917
Private	Ball	A	10/12/1916
Private	Ball	E	03/10/1917
Private	Barclay	G S	04/10/1917
Private	Barker	C	07/10/1917
Private	Barker	J	23/11/1918
Private	Barnacle	G H	18/04/1918
Private	Barnett	F	11/09/1916
Private	Barratt	T	27/07/1917
Private	Barton	W	04/02/1918
Private	Battisson	J	04/10/1916
Serjeant	Baugh	D	11/06/1917
Private	Baxter	H A	27/07/1917

Private	Baynes	S I	29/09/1916
Private	Beamond	J W	04/10/1917
Private	Beard	A	07/10/1918
Serjeant	Beasley	N	27/09/1916
Private	Beck	F	04/10/1917
Private	Beddows	J H	09/09/1916
Private	Beeby	J A	17/07/1917
Private	Bellfield	H E	21/11/1917
Lance Corporal	Bennett	G W	16/12/1916
Private	Bentley	W	26/09/1916
Private	Beresford	J G H	26/08/1917
Corporal	Bevington	F	25/07/1917
Private	Bickley	W	01/10/1916
Private	Bickley	J	27/07/1917
Private	Bill	J	16/08/1917
Private	Bills	W H	18/08/1916
Serjeant	Birch	W P	21/11/1916
Private	Bircher	J	16/08/1917
Private	Bird	W J	27/07/1917
Private	Bird	C J	21/11/1917
Corporal	Bleasdale	A C	27/11/1916
Corporal	Blood	R	13/12/1916
Private	Blundell	A	27/11/1916
Private	Boardman	H	04/10/1917
Private	Body	H C	12/11/1917
Private	Bolton	L	27/07/1917
Private	Bond	A	28/08/1917
Private	Bradley	G W	24/10/1917
Private	Bradshaw	F	19/08/1917
Private	Brant	S T	16/12/1917
Private	Brayshaw	J	08/11/1918
Private	Breen	L	21/11/1917
Private	Broadhurst	C	09/06/1917
Lance Corporal	Brooks	C	08/10/1917
Private	Brown	W	28/09/1916

Private	Brown	W L	08/06/1917
Lance Serjeant	Brown	W H	04/10/1917
Private	Bumby	F A	04/10/1917
Private	Burley	W J	16/12/1916
Corporal	Burrows	A L	23/11/1916
Private	Burton	A	23/11/1916
Second Lieutenant	Bussy	J	20/09/1916
Private	Buttrick	C	04/10/1917
Private	Byfield	W T	25/11/1916
Private	Byrnes	E	19/08/1917
Private	Caswell	A	20/03/1918
Private	Cattle	W	26/03/1916
Private	Challoner	E J	30/09/1916
Second Lieutenant	Chapman	S G	28/09/1916
Captain	Charlton	R	05/10/1917
Captain	Christian	E C	11/09/1916
Private	Churm	W	27/07/1917
Private	Clark	D	28/07/1917
Serjeant	Clay	F W	30/09/1916
Private	Claydon	W	04/10/1917
Private	Clowes	H	08/10/1918
Private	Coleman	D P	25/07/1917
Private	Colledge	A	08/06/1917
Private	Collins	H	27/09/1916
Private	Collins	L	25/05/1918
Private	Collison	S J	17/08/1917
Private	Cooper	S	05/04/1916
Private	Cooper	J	27/09/1916
Private	Cooper	J	06/05/1918
Private	Corns	C	15/01/1918
Private	Cox	S J R	08/06/1917
Private	Cox	A W E	21/11/1917
Lance Corporal	Cox	G H	30/08/1918
Second Lieutenant	Coxe	E N	09/06/1917
Company Serjeant Major	Craddock	T C	06/05/1918

Private	Craw	R H S	01/09/1918
Private	Crawford	W	04/10/1917
Private	Creamer	J W	20/05/1918
Corporal	Crick	B	17/07/1917
Private	Crofts	H	30/08/1918
Private	Cunliffe	G	06/11/1918
Private	Dainty	W	21/08/1918
Private	Dames	L	14/10/1918
Private	Davies	J	02/10/1916
Private	Davies	F	18/07/1917
Private	Davies	L H	27/07/1917
Private	Davies	G	14/11/1917
Private	Davis	J T	24/07/1916
Lance Corporal	Davis	S	27/07/1917
Private	Dawson	F E	01/05/1917
Private	Dean	G	04/06/1917
Private	Dean	E	16/12/1917
Private	Devney	J	24/10/1917
Private	Dickens	A	03/10/1918
Private	Dixon	G	30/09/1916
Lance Corporal	Doyle	I	04/10/1917
Corporal	Drew	C T	28/09/1916
Private	Duffield	J	10/09/1916
Private	Duke	J W	21/11/1917
Private	Dyer	A J	27/09/1916
Private	Eaborne	W	27/07/1917
Private	Eaglestone	P N	31/08/1918
Private	Eccleston	P A	10/02/1918
Private	Edwards	S	23/11/1916
Private	Edwards	S	25/07/1917
Private	Edwards	G R	19/11/1917
Company Quartermaster Serjeant	Edwards	A	05/11/1918
Private	Elliman	E H	01/11/1917
Lance Corporal	Fairbrother	H	26/09/1916

Lance Corporal	Fairfield	T	24/11/1916
Company Quartermaster Serjeant	Fake	E	05/11/1918
Private	Fallon	M	10/09/1916
Lance Corporal	Farr	H O	04/10/1917
Private	Farrell	J	09/10/1917
Private	Fellows	G	10/12/1917
Private	Fereday	J	25/07/1917
Private	Ferguson	J	28/09/1916
Private	Ferneyhough	F	10/06/1917
Private	Field	T	04/10/1917
Corporal	Fisher	J	14/12/1917
Private	Fletcher	I	01/12/1916
Private	Fletcher	W	09/06/1917
Private	Flintham	J	03/10/1917
Lance Corporal	Foster	E R	21/11/1917
Private	Franks	R	19/08/1917
Private	Freeman	E	01/09/1918
Private	Frost	T W	20/12/1917
Private	Gamble	A	18/07/1917
Private	Gamston	W J	23/11/1916
Private	Garbett	J	27/07/1917
Serjeant	Gardiner	F	04/10/1917
Private	Genner	A	07/08/1917
Private	Gibbons	M	14/07/1916
Private	Gibbs	E C	08/06/1917
Private	Gillespie	F	12/11/1917
Private	Glaze	J T	16/12/1916
Lance Corporal	Glover	G	27/07/1917
Private	Glover	T	27/07/1917
Private	Grainger	A	11/01/1917
Private	Grazier	G H B	13/11/1916
Private	Green	C	27/07/1917
Private	Green	J G	08/10/1917
Private	Gretton	S	27/07/1917

Private	Griffiths	A	11/06/1917
Private	Griffiths	A	05/10/1918
Private	Guest	G W	09/06/1917
Lance Corporal	Halgarth	C H	09/06/1917
Private	Hall	T	04/10/1917
Private	Hall	J G	10/10/1917
Corporal	Hancock	A	27/09/1916
Private	Hancock	W	30/11/1917
Private	Handley	F	25/07/1917
Lance Corporal	Handley	J	20/08/1917
Private	Harris	S T	08/06/1917
Private	Harris	W E	09/06/1917
Private	Harris	J	12/11/1917
Private	Harrison	T	27/07/1917
Private	Harvey	J	06/10/1916
Private	Harvey	J A	04/10/1917
Private	Hattersley	F	01/10/1916
Private	Hawkins	T E	07/07/1917
Private	Hawley	G	27/07/1917
Private	Hawley	J	04/10/1918
Private	Haworth	J R	21/11/1916
Private	Hayward	H H	27/07/1917
Private	Haywood	H G	27/07/1917
Private	Haywood	J	05/02/1918
Corporal	Hendley	P J R	19/08/1917
Corporal	Henshaw	J H	01/08/1917
Private	Higginson	W	27/07/1917
Private	Hill	A	08/06/1917
Private	Hill	B	23/07/1917
Private	Hill	A E	04/10/1917
Lance Corporal	Hill	G A	20/05/1918
Private	Hill	F G	07/10/1918
Private	Hodson	G W	14/12/1917
Private	Holland	W	21/11/1917
Private	Holmes	W H	19/02/1918

Private	Holt	W	23/11/1916
Corporal	Horton	H A	04/10/1917
Private	Housley	A	04/10/1917
Private	Howard	F	13/11/1918
Private	Hughes	A	01/10/1916
Private	Hughes	J O	21/11/1917
Private	Hughes	C H	25/04/1918
Private	Hunt	W H	04/10/1917
Private	Hunt	T E	28/06/1918
Lance Corporal	Hutchinson	A	17/08/1917
Private	Inman	C W	25/10/1917
Private	Inskip	F	31/07/1917
Second Lieutenant	Instone	E L	04/08/1917
Private	Jackson	B	28/11/1916
Private	Jackson	R D	04/10/1917
Serjeant	Jackson	J H	03/10/1918
Corporal	Jenkins	J E	30/09/1916
Private	Jennings	H	27/07/1917
Private	Johnson	S	14/07/1916
Private	Jones	E	27/11/1916
Private	Jones	G	29/11/1916
Lance Corporal	Jones	W	08/06/1917
Private	Jones	W A	06/10/1917
Private	Jones	J E	21/11/1917
Lance Corporal	Jones	C	10/10/1918
Private	Keay	F	25/05/1918
Corporal	Keber	F	10/09/1916
Private	Kemp	A	16/06/1918
Private	Kendall	R	28/09/1916
Private	Kenealy	S	10/12/1916
Private	Kilcast	G	07/10/1918
Serjeant	Kirton	F	01/09/1918
Private	Lane	A W	27/09/1916
Private	Lane	E	12/10/1917
Private	Langstone	J	09/06/1917

Private	Lappage	F	30/07/1916
Lance Corporal	Lawley	J	06/09/1916
Private	Leary	G	21/11/1916
Private	Lee	E E	30/09/1916
Lance Corporal	Leech	J	23/11/1916
Private	Lees	A	27/07/1917
Private	Liggins	L	04/10/1917
Private	Linfoot	J	27/07/1917
Private	Lowndes	H B	10/10/1918
Private	Maiden	H	06/09/1916
Lance Corporal	Manford	W	28/03/1918
Private	Mann	J H	21/08/1917
Private	Marchant	A	04/10/1917
Private	Mardle	C K	09/11/1918
Second Lieutenant	Marshall	C	27/07/1917
Private	Mcdermott	T	05/11/1918
Company Serjeant Major	Mcgrath	M	19/08/1917
Private	Meeson	B	09/12/1917
Private	Miller	T H	21/10/1917
Private	Millward	G	22/09/1916
Private	Milton	A J	04/10/1917
Private	Moore	A	04/10/1917
Private	Moreton	A	30/09/1916
Private	Morgan	A	04/10/1917
Lance Serjeant	Morgan	A	10/10/1918
Private	Morris	H	25/04/1917
Private	Mullarkey	J	19/07/1917
Corporal	Navin	J	07/11/1918
Private	Newbury	R	30/09/1916
Private	Norgrove	B	30/09/1916
Private	Norton	A	20/12/1917
Private	Oliver	G	30/09/1916
Private	Onion	J	14/10/1916
Private	Opie	J	27/07/1917
Private	Organ	L	11/09/1916

Private	Owen	J E	22/03/1918
Private	Pam	J	25/07/1917
Lance Corporal	Pardoe	G T	25/07/1917
Private	Pardoe	A	06/05/1918
Lance Corporal	Parker	T C	21/11/1917
Private	Parkes	W H	19/07/1917
Private	Parrish	G H	14/12/1917
Private	Parry	B	26/09/1916
Private	Partridge	S A	27/11/1916
Private	Pascall	L	30/11/1916
Private	Payne	E	03/10/1916
Private	Payne	L	07/10/1918
Private	Peakman	H	04/10/1917
Private	Pearson	H	10/10/1918
Lance Corporal	Peart	J	12/10/1917
Private	Pepper	H	22/08/1918
Lance Corporal	Petty	W	27/09/1916
Private	Pexton	G	27/07/1917
Private	Phillips	W A	21/11/1916
Private	Phipps	J	27/09/1916
Private	Pitt	W H	06/10/1917
Private	Pitt	J	14/12/1917
Private	Plant	D	30/09/1916
Corporal	Plant	W	20/03/1918
Private	Potts	G	09/06/1917
Private	Poulton	W	25/08/1917
Private	Powell	S	29/10/1916
Private	Powell	E	19/08/1917
Private	Powell	S	12/11/1917
Private	Preston	A	08/10/1917
Private	Price	J	06/09/1916
Private	Price	A	30/09/1916
Lance Serjeant	Price	R	07/08/1917
Private	Pugh	L W	09/09/1916
Private	Pye	A	19/08/1917

Private	Rabone	J T	25/05/1918
Private	Richards	G	26/03/1917
Private	Richards	W	18/04/1918
Private	Rilett	H	25/02/1918
Private	Riley	H	29/04/1917
Private	Roberts	H	16/12/1916
Private	Robertshaw	B	04/10/1917
Private	Robinson	C	11/01/1917
Private	Robinson	R A	19/11/1918
Private	Rochelle	G	30/09/1916
Lance Serjeant	Rosewarne	A	19/08/1917
Private	Rouston	H L	13/11/1918
Private	Rowling	F	20/12/1917
Private	Rudge	H	29/09/1916
Private	Rushton	J T	28/09/1916
Private	Russell	J	21/11/1916
Lance Corporal	Sanders	F	21/11/1917
Private	Sandles	J	26/11/1916
Private	Saunders	A H F	14/12/1917
Private	Saunders	S E	10/03/1918
Private	Sawbridge	H	11/01/1917
Private	Sconce	S H	30/09/1916
Private	Scotton	J	16/12/1917
Private	Sharman	F	20/09/1918
Lance Corporal	Sharp	J H	25/07/1917
Private	Sharratt	A	18/08/1917
Private	Shaw	J	27/07/1917
Lance Corporal	Shaylor	S R	10/06/1918
Private	Shemwell	W H	18/05/1916
Lance Corporal	Shepherd	G T	23/11/1916
Private	Shipley	L	04/10/1917
Private	Simpson	W	27/07/1917
Private	Skidmore	W	04/10/1917
Private	Slatter	L A	11/01/1917
Private	Smallwood	G F	28/09/1916

Corporal	Smawley	G E	27/07/1917
Private	Smith	J	24/11/1916
Private	Smith	P	27/09/1916
Private	Smith	P	28/11/1916
Private	Smith	G	09/06/1917
Lance Corporal	Smith	C H	16/08/1917
Private	Smith	F E	04/10/1917
Private	Smith	H T	04/10/1917
Corporal	Smith	A	21/11/1917
Private	Smith	A A	09/03/1918
Lance Corporal	Smith	J W	25/08/1918
Private	Smith	G	28/11/1918
Serjeant	Spencer	J	11/11/1917
Second Lieutenant	Stanway	G	05/10/1917
Private	Steele	A	27/11/1916
Private	Stephenson	M	30/06/1917
Private	Stokes	W	16/12/1916
Private	Street	F	06/09/1916
Private	Suffolk	O W	09/04/1917
Private	Suley	D T	21/11/1916
Private	Sutton	G	21/11/1916
Private	Sutton	T	14/12/1917
Private	Swann	L	08/10/1918
Private	Taylor	J T	06/09/1916
Private	Taylor	A	27/09/1916
Private	Taylor	A	12/01/1917
Lieutenant	Taylor	R C	04/10/1917
Serjeant	Taylor	J	04/10/1917
Lance Corporal	Terry	E	09/06/1917
Private	Thompson	F	07/06/1917
Corporal	Thompson	G E	20/05/1918
Private	Tighe	S	09/06/1917
Private	Till	F	30/09/1916
Private	Tilley	J T	09/06/1917
Second Lieutenant	Tinkler	G H	25/04/1917

Private	Todd	A	09/06/1917
Private	Tomkins	J	04/10/1918
Lance Serjeant	Tuck	J L	23/11/1916
Private	Tuck	A	26/08/1918
Private	Turner	W	09/09/1916
Private	Turner	H	25/09/1916
Private	Turner	C J	27/07/1917
Private	Turner	T	04/10/1917
Private	Twells	J	07/10/1918
Private	Twigg	C	27/07/1916
Private	Underwood	W J	27/07/1917
Serjeant	Vale	W T	05/10/1918
Private	Vale	F	20/11/1918
Second Lieutenant	Vaughan	G W	21/11/1917
Private	Walker	F A	04/10/1917
Private	Wall	W	08/06/1917
Lance Serjeant	Wallis	G M	04/10/1917
Private	Walters	A	27/09/1916
Private	Walton	J E	28/11/1917
Lance Corporal	Ward	J	02/04/1916
Private	Ward	T	21/11/1916
Private	Warrender	J E G	02/10/1916
Private	Wastell	H	03/10/1917
Private	Waterhouse	C	08/10/1918
Serjeant	Watts	J	04/10/1917
Private	Weaver	J T	09/06/1917
Private	Weaver	W J	07/10/1918
Private	Webb	B	04/10/1917
Private	Webb	R	10/10/1918
Private	Weston	J	09/06/1917
Private	Weston	P	07/10/1918
Private	White	W R	10/01/1917
Lieutenant	White	E V	06/09/1918
Corporal	Williams	T	11/01/1917
Lance Corporal	Williams	L	04/10/1917

Private	Williams	T H	12/10/1917
Private	Williams	W	15/10/1918
Private	Wilson	H G	21/03/1918
Private	Wilson	O	24/03/1918
Private	Wood	A E	04/10/1917
Private	Wood	J W	06/02/1918
Corporal	Woodhouse	J W	27/11/1916
Captain	Worcester	H P	10/09/1916
Private	Wright	S	27/09/1916
Private	Wright	J	18/07/1917
Private	Wyke	J	29/09/1916
Private	Yarranton	A	21/11/1917
Lance Corporal	Yates	G	27/07/1917
Serjeant	Yates	E	20/12/1917
Lance Corporal	Yates	E	03/08/1918
Corporal	York	E H	27/09/1916
Private	Youngjohns	A	19/08/1918

Annex G - Lt Col W H Carter
Commanding Officer 7th Battalion South Staffordshire Regiment

Harry Carter was born on 1 April 1879 at Wolverhampton, the son of William John Carter, a gas tube maker, and his wife Annie, nee Dingley. The 1891 census showed he was the eldest of seven children, and educated at St Luke's, Blakenhall, before taking employment as a gas tube worker. William Carter, known as Harry, enlisted in the British Army at Wolverhampton on 20 December 1899 (aged 20 years, 9 months), on a seven-year engagement plus five years in the Reserves. He was attested into the 2nd Battalion South Staffordshire Regiment; his service record shows him as small in stature being 5 feet 4¾ inches tall, weighing 8 stones 3 pounds, with a 34 inch chest.

After initial recruit training at the Regimental Depot from 20 December 1899 to 29 May 1900, he was temporarily drafted to the 1st Battalion for the South Africa Campaign until 21 October 1902. Here Private Carter saw active service in the Boer War; he was the recipient of the Queen's South Africa Medal with Cape Colony, Orange Free State, and Transvaal Clasps, and the King's South Africa Medal with 1901 and 1902 Clasps. On 11 August 1901 he was promoted to Lance Corporal.

Following the end of hostilities, Harry Carter resumed peacetime activities with the 2nd Battalion, soldiering in India from 22 October 1902 to 28 November 1907. This was followed by further service in South Africa until 15 February 1911, when the Battalion returned to England. Whilst in India he was promoted to the rank of Corporal in 1906, and Lance Sergeant the following year. In South Africa, after passing an Assistant Signalling Instructors Course, he was advanced to Sergeant rank on 22 March 1910.

In the United Kingdom the 2nd Battalion of the South Staffs was based at Lichfield between 1911-1913, and at Aldershot from 1913 until the outbreak of the Greart War. On 12 August 1914 the Battalion embarked for Le Havre as part of 6th Brigade, 2nd Division, in Douglas Haig's I Corps. At this juncture Harry Carter was the Battalion Signals Sergeant.

As with the majority of the BEF, the 2nd Battalion South Staffs Regiment was heavily engaged in the Battle of Mons, taking part in the Retreat from Mons including rear guard actions at Landrecies and Villers-Cotteret. This was just a foretaste of the severe fighting that was to follow. The 2nd South Staffs War Diary records their involvement during the Battles of the Marne (7 -10 September), the Aisne (12-15 September) and First Ypres (19 October - 22 November) particularly Langemarck, Gheluvelt and Nonne Boschen.

Prior to the outbreak of the First World War, peacetime promotion for both officers and other ranks was very slow. Harry Carter was obviously an efficient and good NCO, but his promotion to substantive Sergeant in 1910 had taken ten years. Stemming the German advance on the Western Front between August and December 1914 decimated much of the operational strength of the BEF, and particularly severe was the loss of junior infantry officers. From November 1914 onwards "officer deaths on the Western Front began to run at the rate of 1 in 7 and officer casualties - that is killed, wounded, missing or taken prisoner - at 1 in 2" (1).

In the British Army during 1913, just seven officers were commissioned from the ranks. In August 1914 alone, five hundred Warrant Officers and NCOs were commissioned. By the end of the war the numbers had risen to 6,713, 41 per cent of the total number of permanent commissions. The contribution made to the British war effort by these individuals is scarcely recognised by the general public, the majority of whom erroneously assumes that officers were exclusively drawn from a public-school background.

Harry Carter was commissioned 2nd Lieutenant in the field on 4 January 1915, and full Lieutenant on 18 June 1915. In the next three years, following rapid promotion, he proved himself to be a superb and highly regarded infantry officer, showing bravery and leadership qualities during some of the heaviest fighting on the Western Front.

On 1 July 1917 he was made a substantive Captain in the Royal Warwickshire Regiment. He returned to duty on the Western Front on 4 July where he reverted to second in command of 13th Essex with the rank of Acting Major. This posting was of a very short duration because, on 19 July 1917 Harry Carter, aged 38, was appointed Acting Lieutenant Colonel as the Commanding Officer of the 7th South Staffordshire Regiment, in 33 Brigade, 11th (Northern) Division. This was an appointment he was to hold for the rest of the war.

11th Division was raised on 21 August 1914 as part of Kitchener's New Army (K1). It served first at Gallipoli, before transferring to the Western Front in 1916, where it gained a reputation as one of the best divisions in the BEF. It performed particularly well at the Third Battle of Ypres [more commonly known as Passchendaele] between 27 July and 9 October 1917 at Langemarck, Polygon Wood, Broodseinde and Poelcapelle, and led the First Army's advance in the autumn of 1918. During this time Major General H R Davies, who had assumed command on 12 May 1917, identified Harry Carter as an indefatigable soldier with superb leadership skills.

Harry Carter's rapid advance from Sergeant to Acting Lieutenant Colonel in a two-year period, together with the award of the MC and DSO, quite naturally drew much praise from the citizens of Wolverhampton and its environs. As a result, on 23 March 1918, he was given a civic reception in Wolverhampton - receiving a silver sword, having his portrait painted and a street named after him (Carter Road in Whitmore Reans, previously Bismarck Road). Perhaps his most satisfying gift was a watch inscribed

"As a token of admiration from his friends in Blakenhall, Wolverhampton, upon gaining high military distinction during the present world war."

The last year of the First World War saw Harry Carter leading his troops with the same verve and determination; on 23 May he was again Mentioned in Despatches, and promoted Brevet Major on 12 June. Between 26 August and 5 November he was involved in the Battles of the Scarpe, Drocourt-Queant, Canal du Nord, Cambrai (1918), the Pursuit to the Selle, the Battle of the Sambre and the Passage of the Grand Honelle. During these battles, Harry Carter continued to be an inspiring leader, a fact which saw him again honoured by the award of a Bar to his DSO, for his actions only two days before the Armistice came into force. This is indicative of the mindset of a front line senior officer determined 'to get the job done'.

The award was announced in the London Gazette dated 2 April 1919, but the citation was not published until Wednesday 10 December (page 15280). It reads:

"Capt and Brevet Major (Temp Lt. Col.) William Henry Carter, DSO, MC, Royal Warwicks Regiment, attached 7th Battalion South Staffs Regiment. "For skilful leading of his battalion during the operations 8th and 9th November, 1918, in the advance from Autrappe to Geognies Chaussee. On 8th November 1918, he by his drive and initiative kept his battalion going forward through enemy opposition and by a personal reconnaissance reported his exact dispositions at the end of the day. He has at all times set a very fine example to those under him."

Military Cross for Wolverhampton Officer.

The King has conferred the Military Cross on Second-Lieutenant William Henry Carter, 2nd South Staffords, for consistent good work throughout the campaign, notably on November 24, 1915. The enemy exploded a mine, killing and wounding most of the garrison. Lieutenant Carter at once started to reorganise the defence of the crater. He was

LIEUTENANT W. H. CARTER.

slightly wounded, but remained at his post, and it was mainly due to his courage and example that two hostile bomb attacks on the crater were repulsed. He also organised a bomb attack on the enemy, thus keeping them quiet while the position was being consolidated.

Second-Lieutenant Carter, who is the son of Mr. W. J. Carter, Maxwell Road, Wolverhampton, has served seventeen years in the army, and went through the Boer war. He went to France last year as a signal sergeant.

FROM PRIVATE TO BRIGADIER

NOW HE IS A FACTORY WORKER

Penn Man's Battle Honours

HIS PEACE JOB PROBLEMS

From Our Own Correspondent
WOLVERHAMPTON, Sunday.

I STOPPED a cyclist at Penn, near Wolverhampton, to-day and asked him where Mr. Carter lived.

"Do you mean the captain?" queried.

"He was a brigadier-general," I cried.

The cyclist pointed to a nearby cottage, and that was how I found Mr. William Henry Carter, once an acting brigadier-general, now on duty at ing works, of Boulton Brothers, Ltd., Wolverhampton.

Mr.—formerly Acting Brigadier-General—W. H. Carter, photographed at his home yesterday with one of his children.

IN 1915

Mr. Carter enlisted at Wolverhampton as a private of 19, in the 7th South Staffords, in 1915. He arrived in the trenches and wounded, and went out with the British Expeditionary Force to France. He was then brigade signals sergeant. For gallant conduct in the field he was given a commission in 1915, and became adjutant.

After a year Mr. Carter was recommended to the rank of temporary major.

When I commented that his progress was pretty rapid, he said: "It happened like this.

"Major Buckley, Wolverhampton Wanderers' centre-half, was at that time second in command of the 5th Middlesex, and he said the C.O. were both wounded shortly before an attack.

"I was sent for to take command of the battalion. Mind you, I had then had 16 or 17 years' service in the Army.

HOME FOR REST

"The C.O., who was only slightly wounded, soon returned, and I then took over the 5th Essex, whose C.O. had been taken ill, and was appointed temporary lieutenant-colonel. I was with them for six months and then came home for three months' rest."

"I was sent out again and took command of the 7th South Staffords. I commanded them till the end of the war, being promoted acting brigadier-general."

It seemed a simple enough account that I mentioned his D.S.O. with bar, and M.C., with bar. "For distinguished service in the field and conspicuous gallantry?"

"And what about the Bronze Cross of St. Stanislaus?"

"As a matter of fact," he continued, "I was recommended for the V.C. for carrying a chap out of the line. But I didn't get the V.C., I got the Military Order.

GRATUITY

"When I was demobilised I received a gratuity of £1,500. I put the money into a poultry farm near Claverley but, but it was not a success. Then I tried ICI, but they were a failure, and so I came to Penn to the bolt works. I split this with my wife and five children. The youngest is five and the oldest sixteen.

"I worked at the J.B.B. works as mechanic for five years, and I shortly before the last Jubilee. Then I went to work at Claverley. A local artist painted me—I think the picture hangs in the Wolseley Memorial Club in Wolverhampton—and during the war I was given a new sovereign.

"And now?"

HAPPY

"Oh, I'm as happy as a king, and as long as I can get work it doesn't"

Annex H – Bibliography

Books

- Ashford. Dr A. H. The History of The Seventh South Staffordshire Regiment. *Boyle, Son and Watchurst.* 1919.
- Jones. H. A The War in The Air. *Claredon Press.* 1931.
- Jones. J. P. The History of The Staffordshire Regiment. 1923.
- Powes. M. Zeppelins Over The Midlands. *Pen and Sword.* 2016.
- Vale. W. L. The History of The Staffordshire Regiment. *Gale & Polden* 1969.

Primary Sources

- The Walsall Local Research Centre
- National Archives
- 7th South Staffordshire Regiment War Diary
- Author personal diary and records of E Mason
- Author documents of T C Craddock and Family

Printed in Great Britain
by Amazon